Studies in Writing & Rhetoric

Other Books in the Studies in Writing & Rhetoric Series

Self-Development and College Writing

Self-Development and College Writing

Nick Tingle

SOUTHERN ILLINOIS UNIVERSITY PRESS

Carbondale

Publication partially funded by a subvention grant from The Conference on College
Composition and Communication of the National Council of Teachers of English.

Library of Congress Cataloging-in-Publication Data
Tingle, Nick, 1945–
Self-development and college writing / Nick Tingle.
    p. cm. — (Studies in writing and rhetoric)
Includes bibliographical references and index.
1. English language—Rhetoric—Study and teaching. 2. Academic writing—Study
and teaching. 3. Self-culture. I. Title. II. Series. III. Studies in writing & rhetoric.
PE1404.T56 2004
808'.042'071—dc22   2004004835
ISBN 0-8093-2580-2 (pbk. : alk. paper)

Printed on recycled paper. ♻

The paper used in this publication meets the minimum requirements of American
National Standard for Information Sciences—Permanence of Paper for Printed
Library Materials, ANSI Z39.48-1992. ∞

To Olga Naud

Contents

Preface

In my more than twenty years of teaching writing (and nothing but writing), I must admit that I have yearned for a time when I might sit down before a stack of seventy-five student papers and feel a Buddha-like calm. I thought I might become inured. Instead I continue to feel anxiety. Part of that distress is due to grading; I just don't like doing it and never will. But there's something else, too. The stack that I am about to dig through is my gold mine. This mining is a tough business; sometimes I hit mostly earth and stone. But sometimes I hit gold.

I don't mean gold in the sense of something beautifully written; I mean it in the sense of finding something—in a turn of phrase, or in the middle of a paragraph, or maybe running through a whole paper—that helps me better to understand the emotional ups and downs, the psychology, of students as they learn and write their way into the academic universe. This insight is gold because in learning more about how students learn, I learn how to teach better. Sometimes it's not much; just a question I hadn't thought to ask and that I will ask next time. But sometimes a whole vista, an entirely different angle opens up, and I learn something not just about teaching but about me as a person who teaches.

So perhaps the anxiety is not entirely a bad thing. Maybe it means that I still approach each class as a mini experiment, or as an exercise in trial and error, or as an attempt to discover something. That's how I try to set up my classes: as environments supportive of experimentation and trial and error, as places where students too might strike gold. And if they don't, and I, in plowing through the papers, hit mostly dirt, I can learn even from that. I was barking up the wrong tree and must readjust.

Whatever else one may take from the following, I hope this central point is clear: the teaching of writing is a significant and meaningful activity. It is and will continue to be so, as long as one sees the teaching of writing as engaging students in a developmental step, and as long as one sees in the activity of teaching potentials for one's own self-development.

Acknowledgments

This product of solitary labor would not have seen the light of day were it not for its readers. I thank Lad Tobin, Bruce Ballenger, and Nancy Welch for their helpful and suggestive commentary. I thank Mark Bracher and Robert Samuels for talking about psychoanalysis and education with me, and Charles "Chuck" Bazerman for getting me off the dime when my writing on pedagogy was stalled. I am most grateful to Robert Brooke, who said that he would guide me through the process. This he did with unstinting, timely, and always supportive response.

And most especially, I thank Carol Press, who has always helped me remember my true self and who is as devoted as I to the ideal of self-development.

Self-Development and College Writing

1 / Psychoanalysis and Development

Richard Nguyen came to the United States from Vietnam when he was ten. He was a senior in my summer school writing class designed for sophomores. When I saw Richard's writing, I understood why he had put off the class. I didn't want to flunk him; my class was one of two he needed for graduation. So I cut a side deal with him. Rather than do the assignments for the class, he could write about himself and his life. But we would have to meet regularly to discuss his writing.

During one of these meetings, I said, "You know, Richard, I understand everything you are saying here. . . ." As I went on to explain myself, Richard, apparently not listening to me at all, said, "You do?"

"Do what?" I wanted to know.

"Understand," he said; and he tapped his paper with his finger to make sure I knew what he was talking about.

"Sure," I said, somewhat puzzled.

I looked at Richard. His eyes were big, and he was very still. At that moment something happened between us. Our relationship had altered in some fundamental way. I don't know exactly how he had seen me before. But now he saw me as someone who, in spite of his many and various problems with the English language, understood what he wrote. That comprehension meant something to him, something deep, something that I, as a native speaker, could never fully appreciate. And something shifted for me, too, when I sensed how important he seemed to feel my understanding was. I no longer felt I was hectoring him; the impatience and sense of frustration went out of my voice. I relaxed.

I would like to be able to report that after this marvelous moment, Richard's writing improved by leaps and bounds. It didn't. Still, I did hear from him the following year. He had graduated and gone on to get a job that involved computers, making more money in his first year than I made after fifteen years of teaching. He wanted to know whether I had any grammar books. He was doing a lot of e-mailing as part of his work, and he said he realized that he needed better to know what a sentence was. He dropped by my office, and I gave him two grammars.

This little story could be interpreted in a couple of ways. First, one might argue that it suggests theorists of activity systems are right. People learn how to write situatedly, in direct and immediate relation, in the case of Richard, to a working environment or, in the case of students generally, in and out of an immediate and situated relation to a particular discipline. This argument has been used to suggest, quite firmly, that courses of the kind I write about here— generic academic writing courses for generic students, not in any particular discipline—are a waste of time, if, that is, one thinks of oneself as teaching writing.

I take from the story, however, a different interpretation. I don't dispute that Richard was clearly learning the conventions of English to perform better in his job. But while I surely do not take all the credit, I believe my moment with Richard may have played a significant role in his self-perception as a writer. My understanding, or more precisely, his experience of feeling that what he wrote was understood, stabilized him relative to this painful activity known as writing the English language. To use the technical language I will more fully explain, I functioned for him as a supportive and affirming selfobject relative to his self-experience as a writer. That he returned a year later for some grammars confirms that Richard perceived me as someone supportive of his move into this new activity system.

The generic academic writing class is far from a waste of time if it is conceived as a transitional space or supportive milieu not for generic students but for persons who are attempting to understand and come to terms with what is being asked of them by the university. I work in a large research university. I would not be so concerned if such places recognized the need to support students in their movement into academia. But they don't. The writing class as transitional space, as a place where students might find some support in their attempts to understand, cannot stop but certainly may inhibit the waste of an education.

In this book, I broadly explain such terms as *transitional space* and *supportive milieu*. I also suggest the importance these ideas have in understanding the critical role of the writing class in education. In this first chapter, I offer a theoretical explanation of these terms and others—such as *narcissism, narcissistic wounding,* and *selfobjects*—by drawing upon the work of Heinz Kohut. I also use the developmental theory of Robert Kegan better to explain the broad outlines of the developmental move students are required to make upon entry into the particular epistemological terrain of the university. In so doing, I also situate my theoretical outlook relative to Lacanism, feminism, and postmodernism, issues more frequently treated in composition and rhetoric studies.

I value theory enormously. It can help clarify and make sense of our experience. But as Kohut says, some theories are "experience distant" and others are "experience near." In the remaining chapters, I bring "near" the theories I examine in the first chapter. In chapter 2, I examine one writing assignment with an eye toward further explicating Kegan's notion of the developmental move from the third to the forth order of consciousness and the narcissistic wounding that I believe necessarily attends this move for students. But, as I insist, the creation of a writing class as transitional space requires the construction of an intersubjective space, one that involves a dialectical relation between the subjectivity of the students and that of the teacher. Accordingly, in chapter 3, I examine writing instructors' psychological allegiances to their "theories," whether consciously retained or not, and suggest the ways such theories do and do not lead to the creation of an intersubjective space. This intersubjective space is elusive, but in the final chapter, drawing on student work, I attempt to evoke it as a horizon that, if perceived, alters the landscape.

Basic Theory: An Overview

The small writing class as transitional space offers a precious opportunity. By conceiving of the writing class as an environment conducive to helping students come to a certain psychological relationship with the activity of writing, a teacher may assist students in finding and developing their particular relationship to the larger academic terrain. The key to the creation of this kind of environment is understanding or, to be more precise, empathy. Empathy is not, of course, exactly the same as understanding. One may understand something purely intellectually, say a problem in math. But Heinz Kohut defines empathy as the means by which a person gains access, both consciously and unconsciously, to the "inward" psychological states of another ("Introspection and Empathy").

There is nothing mysterious about empathy. It happens all the time. One has a feeling about what someone else is feeling. The closer people are in terms of background and culture, the more they are automatically inclined to know through empathy what another person is feeling. One brother may know better than any other person what the other brother is feeling. But as these examples make clear, one's capacity for empathy is determined and thus limited by one's particular social and cultural background. One's particular psychological configuration too may limit the range of one's empathy. Optimistic people, for example, may be more automatically attuned to happy states and have difficulty understanding darker moods.

One may feel indeed that one has come to know another person and then, with something of a shock, realize that one really knows nothing about his or her deeper psychological states. After twenty years of marriage, one or both partners in the relationship may realize that they really don't understand each other. Such a realization can, but need not, end the relationship. The range of a person's empathy can be expanded, but such expansion requires a kind of work, a labor. The conscious exercise of empathy requires, Kohut says, *vicarious introspection.* In effect, expanding the range of one's empathy requires that one become, if not precisely conscious of, at least vaguely aware of how one's background, circumstances, and psychological configuration may limit, willy-nilly, one's understanding or empathetic grasp of the psychological states of another. Knowing another involves knowing oneself.

One tool for the expansion of empathy—there are others—that I have found most useful as a person and as a teacher is psychoanalysis as it appears in the self psychology of Heinz Kohut and in the object relations of D. W. Winnicott. I have more to say about these theories later, but for the present, I emphasize that I do not take these theories as granting me privileged access to the real. Rather I accept, with Winnicott, that no person is in direct contact with reality. One has rather diverse and complex relationships to the real. A theory is one such relationship. As a relationship, a theory necessarily shapes the reality it represents. It discovers what it creates and creates what it discovers.

The only way to test a psychological theory about another's self-states is to apply it and see whether the one to whom it is applied feels that he or she has been empathetically understood and to what degree. In this light, a psychoanalytic theory is probably best understood as an interpretive tool. The theory as interpretive tool necessarily foregrounds certain aspects or domains of the other's psychological reality or subjectivity. The other, however, may experience his or her self as not having been understood exactly because the theory foregrounds certain aspects of the self at the expense of others.

This misunderstanding means not that one throws out one's theory lock, stock, and barrel but only that one again begins to think about it and the implications of it for the way one conceives and interacts with the subjectivities of others. Psychoanalytic theories are not simply theories about reality; they are also theories about practice. All psychological theories carry with them, sometimes implicitly, sometimes explicitly, what might be called an ethics, a series of rules or directives about how to best achieve one's goal. The theory, in short, offers not simply access to the real but also guidelines for those actions or that practice most likely to achieve that reality.

This description might appear to be a self-fulfilling prophecy of the most self-delusional kind were it not for the fact that the steps don't always work or that they create something one hadn't expected.

Because the object of psychoanalytic theory is the human subject, psychoanalysis is not an exact science but a historical one. People change as social, economic, and historical conditions change, and as people change, so do the ways they experience themselves at the deepest levels of the self. Not only does psychoanalysis, as theory or relation to the real, create what it discovers, but what it takes as the object of its study, the human psyche in all its manifestations, is changing, as Marx might have it, "behind its back."

If one is wedded to an empirical notion of objective truth, this conclusion might appear appalling. I find it liberating, for it points directly to the one place where knowledge might still be located: in the selves of particular individuals. If, as I believe, the self is a series or congeries or an agglutination of diverse conscious and unconscious relations to the real, one may still work at knowing exactly these relations. The goal of this knowing, however, is not truth as something *out there* but truth as something very much *in here,* as the vitalizing, realistic, and workable relationship between who one is and what one does, between one's being and one's doing. This "truth" is not something abstract but something very useful to the individual. Only if one is able to establish this relationship can one hope, in the face of life's vicissitudes, to continue to develop throughout the span of a life and to experience oneself over that span as a continuum.

Kohut defines psychological health as functioning in accord with one's design. I think this a marvelous definition. When I praise my cat, as I frequently do, for its "catness," when I teasingly ask it where it found a tailor able to make it such a smoothly fitting coat, I praise it, in effect, for functioning in accord with its design. For human beings, however, functioning in accord with one's design may represent as much an ideal as an achieved actuality. Indeed, Kohut argues that the central pathology of our times may be the fragmented self—the self that has lost contact with its design, with that which allows it to cohere and to exist as a continuum through time (*Restoration,* 285–90). More important for my purposes here, the course of a normal development necessarily means losing touch at least momentarily with one's design as one attempts in the lived present to reassert a different or changed relation to that design.

As a child learns to walk, he or she necessarily falls down. The person in his or her middle age must also adjust to the exigencies of that developmental phase. Some youthful ambitions may have to be relinquished, not without mourning, and one's hopes redefined on a new and different footing. And, as I argue throughout the following, students in entering the university engage an environment that may or may not excite in them a developmental move, one involving a potential destabilization of self toward the goal of reintegration of self with design.

This developmental move is not, of course, the same as learning to walk or reaching middle age. Both of these moves are impelled by the particular genetic makeup of human beings. The developmental move that students may undertake while at the university is not so impelled. Rather, it is enjoined by the social structures of the university, by the particular ways that institution presents and conceives of knowledge. Students inevitably feel, consciously sometimes but most frequently unconsciously, the pressure of this environment. But whether they undertake the developmental move enjoined by that environment is another matter completely.

This movement not only is unimpelled but also is fraught with difficulties for the person who undertakes it. The writing class as transitional environment serves two developmental purposes. First, it may invite students to make the developmental move by pointing to the value of it, and second, and just as important, it may support students if they are drawn into making the move. Indeed, in practice, these two purposes are not distinct. The more the writing class clarifies the value, the more students, as they come to understand it, experience destabilization at their current level of development. As a transitional environment, however, the writing class may acknowledge and support students in their moments of destabilization and uncertainty.

More specific, the developmental move requires that students assume toward their already existing epistemologies a different form of self-relation. These epistemologies are best described as a complex of relations that involve beliefs, ideas, ethical principles, thoughts, notions, and basic affective attitudes toward reality. Forming a new self-relation to these things requires that students move through an intermediate stage of doubt and skepticism about their already-in-place epistemologies. Or to use the language of Heinz Kohut, students' already-in-place ideals, ideas, beliefs, and commonsense notions serve them, at the level of cognition, as stabilizing selfobjects.

A selfobject, for Kohut, is a person, place, thing, or activity that is conducive to a person's sense of psychological stability or centeredness, no matter how momentary or provisional. My computer, for example, is just an object, a mysterious complex of plastic and electricity; but it functions for me also as a selfobject. When it is on the blink, I feel irritated, at times even angry. When some mornings I have pushed the power button and nothing at all appears on the screen, I have experienced anxiety, even a loss of purpose. What am I going to do now? When the computer is operating well, it functions as a supportive selfobject. It assists me in my plan of action, and I am scarcely aware of it as an external object (a mysterious complex of plastic and electronics) at all.

To be clear, while all selfobjects promote in the individual psyche a feeling of coherence or stability, one may make a broad distinction between good selfobjects and bad ones. Roughly, one may say a good selfobject, while lending coherence, also serves the goal of continued self-development. A bad selfobject, however, serves the defensive purpose not of developing but of protecting the self against destabilization by relatively archaic and disruptive wants or needs.

Again, the computer may serve as an example. As a bad selfobject, it may provide me with momentary coherence, but the energy expended in maintaining this coherence may amount to pouring good money after bad. My relationship to the computer as selfobject may be primarily addictive or compulsive. The computer, again, is just an object, a complex of plastic and electronics, but it functions as selfobject and, in this instance, as a bad one because my self-relationship to it is bad, or nondevelopmental.

I attempt to build into the creation of the writing class as transitional environment the possibility, at least, that students will experience the activity of writing as a good selfobject, one that stabilizes and furthers the developmental move enjoined by the university.

The activity of writing, as stabilizing, may support students as they undergo the destabilization inherent in the developmental move. More specific, as I have suggested, the movement into the structures of the university and into a comprehension of its view of knowledge requires that students question or call into doubt their beliefs. This doubt or questioning is not simply a matter of intellection; rather it requires that the individual alter in a significant way his or her self-relation to knowledge, what it is, and how it is constituted.

The mind and the body, the psyche and the soma, the intellect and the affects are not distinct. Ideas, thoughts, beliefs, and the massive realm of common sense all may act for individuals as stabilizing selfobjects, as things taken as existing in the world, that affirm and give substance to a particular psychological configuration of self. Questioning these objects can and frequently does destabilize the self. This destabilization is central to the developmental move enjoined by the university: to question, to doubt, to look critically at all that one thought one knew and took for granted. The enjoining of this movement, though frequently unacknowledged and largely unformulated, I take to be the central and most important educative purpose of the modern, secular research university.

I will have more to say about the exact nature of the developmental move. For now, I can say that whether students make this critical move is pretty much a hit-or-miss, sink-or-swim affair. Some few students get it; most don't. Most don't get it because the pedagogy of the university works against acknowledging even the move itself, as a psychological transition, and thus is ill-positioned to offer the kind of psychological support students could use in making it. That is one reason I believe the writing class, the one aimed especially at students in their first year, is important. It is possible to do things in those classes that are simply impossible anywhere else.

I would not have bothered with Richard Nguyen at all if I had been teaching a class of two hundred. I probably would have flunked him. I didn't because I had the chance to speak with him, learn a little about him, and see he was really a hardworking person from a culture quite different from mine. He knew computers inside and out, having taught himself for the most part. He had to suffer a toothache for a whole weekend because, without money, he had to wait to see the dentist in student health services. He knew Vietnamese, English, and French, and was going that summer to France to spend some time with the young woman that his family had arranged for him to marry.

We had the chance at least for a special moment. I don't even know what made me say, "I understand everything you are saying here." Perhaps something like empathy had been working. Because it seems such an obvious thing to say, perhaps I assumed he already knew it, knew that I was complaining only about the host of little things that got in the way of my being able to understand him quickly. But he apparently hadn't known that I grasped his meaning. And when he did know it, and understood that I understood, everything shifted. I saw this person would learn. And he saw that he no longer had to feel he made no sense at all and was better positioned then to tackle the host of little things, one at a time.

My Situation and Its Implications

Before I explicate, in the next section, my particular pedagogical theories, I offer a few words about who I might be. I believe all writing is autobiographical, in the sense that it is always informed at some level by the narcissism of the particular author. The particularities of the author, though, are frequently buried in much academic writing. I state explicitly some of my particularities, hoping that such a statement might prove useful in understanding what follows or in attempting to answer the question, "Where is this person coming from?"

Perhaps most important, I come to this project as a teacher of writing. This work is what I have done for more than twenty-five years. When I say "teacher of writing," that is precisely what I mean. I have not taught graduate students theories of composition, nor have I taught literature. I have taught writing to largely first- and second-year students. I have taught seven to eight, on average, classes of writing per year. I have been fortunate to have done so in an employment and institution that, compared with the employment and institutional situations of many teachers of writing, have been relatively supportive. I have, for example, my own office, my own telephone, and my own computer. I do not take these things for granted because, while my situation is relatively supportive, I have been employed for more than 20 years under the official job classification of lecturer. I do not have tenure. I was employed for my first eight years on one-year contracts and since that time on renewable three-year contracts.

There is much embedded in these particularities, and there are a number of reasons why I believe they are worth mentioning. In what follows, I offer an unremitting criticism of education as I believe it is performed, or rather not performed, by the larger institutional situation—that of a moderate-sized research institution—in which I work. Were I a fully tenured member of the institution, I strongly doubt I would be so unremitting in my criticism. Or, let us say, were I to be critical, I expect I would be so on grounds different from those I offer here.

Within the institution as a teacher of writing, I am a relative outsider in more than one way. Most significantly, though, I am a teacher and not a researcher. I am not fully embedded within any particular disciplinary terrain. My job as a teacher of writing does not involve me in passing to my students a body of knowledge that they must know if they are to begin to know a discipline in general. In this way, my position as outsider has been fruitful. It has allowed me to think about and develop a notion of pedagogy and education that I doubt would have been *as* visible to me at least had I taught from and within particular disciplinary constraints.

The downside of this notion is that it has cemented my status as outsider. When I try to speak to tenured faculty about my concerns, I have a strong feeling that many don't have the foggiest notion what I am talking about. While acknowledging problems, they claim that the university, with its current resources, is doing the best it can to educate. Given their position, my tenured colleagues are ill-prepared to understand that the university is not educating.

Experiences of this kind—including walking into a classroom where the seats are bolted to the floor—have made me feel excluded and not affirmed in my particular narcissistically charged aims and goals. Consequently, I experience, nearly daily, moments of anxiety and disillusionment. Anxiety arises even when I read in the one area of knowledge (aside from psychoanalytic theory) that I know best: composition studies and theory. In such readings, I anticipate, at least, some affirmation of my particular experiential realities; instead, to borrow a phrase from Heinz Kohut, I experience these theories as too frequently "experience distant."

During such moments, I may personally and experientially participate in the conflict described by Kurt Spellmeyer as a split in the profession of composition studies, not between theory and practice per se but between "two different versions of professional authority": the text-based authority of composition theorists and the experience-based knowledge of writing teachers (427). My anxiety may arise, then, from a sense of tornness, of not quite fitting into the profession that best represents my interests and reflects my concerns.

Certainly what follows will suggest that I belong to the camp of writing teachers rather than writing theorists. I draw a great deal from my experience as a teacher (and as a person). But, I hasten to add, I know "for example" isn't proof, whether the example comes from the newspaper or from one's personal experience. Rather, I hope through the explication of what I have experienced as a teacher of writing to better explain my general theory, and I hope to affirm the experience of other instructors of writing. But however I may intend to use my personal experience, I do not doubt that some of the criticism I direct at various theories of composition or, more precisely, at the psychological function such theories may serve for teachers of writing arises from my sense of these theories as experience distant.

What follows is rife with theory. In fact, what I have to say would not have been possible without psychoanalytic theory. Psychoanalysis is not, of course, monolithic; some forms of it I don't like at all. That I am drawn to theories that emphasize the notion of self and self-development is not an accident. Here again, the particularities of my experience may help in understanding where I am coming from.

I am a first-generation college student. I was the first and, I believe, only member of my immediate family line to receive a PhD. My family of origin is working-class and, during the years of my childhood, rural and agrarian. I lived in a small community in the deep South. Now I find myself a member of the professional classes. I approached this class position as an outsider; moreover my movement to this position was marked by disjuncture. I have been and continue to be deeply involved in making sense out of and holding together the various stories I tell myself about who I am. Psychoanalysis tells me I will never know the whole story. It also tells me that one can never escape one's most deeply buried past, as it continues to live in the unconscious. Trying to tell the story remains important as a way of asserting a continuum between where one is and where one came from.

My personal experience within higher education has been marked by disjuncture, socially and intellectually. In the long run at least, my exposure to the theories and epistemologies of the university have been self-affirming; they have allowed me to make sense of things in ways I otherwise could not. But my path to understanding theory and how it might work to stabilize the self—how it might act as a relation to the real—was not easy. To put the matter rather abstractly, I experienced the intellectual development enjoined of me by education as very much an emotional and psychological experience. At moments of particular crisis and uncertainty, I had even, as it were, my own battle cry drawn from Hegel. "You are," I would tell myself, "experiencing the labor of the negative."

My theory of the writing classroom as transitional environment is rooted in the particularities of my experience. It represents an extension of my sense of self-continuum. One might consider it simply a self-projection, but I don't think so. I believe the university and its ways of knowing do enjoin of students a developmental move, one fraught with potentials for destabilization. True, most students that I teach are not first-generation college students; many indeed do not even see getting a college education as a choice. Instead, they have simply been socialized, in a way I was not, into the idea of obtaining one.

All that this socialization means, however, is that students' experience of destabilization remains relatively unconscious. The relatively more dramatic disjuncture involved in my movement into education forced me to become more conscious of my self-experience; this consciousness was necessary if I were to preserve a continuum of self. That many of my students are not involved in negotiating such a dramatic disjuncture, particularly relative to social station, does not mean they are not experiencing disruptions at the levels of cognition or intellection, or that they do not experience the necessity, albeit at unconscious levels, of locating and maintaining a sense of self-continuum.

These remarks on my self-particularity may suggest that I do not claim professional authority wholly on the basis of my experience-based knowledge as a writing teacher. My claims rest on something far deeper than my experiences as a teacher of writing. Indeed, I wonder whether I would even have any experiences as a teacher of writing, ones at least that I might be able to formulate or make sense of, were it not for the ways that these experiences are shaped and determined by my experience as a person. This question no doubt rests at the bottom of my belief that students too, if they are to garner the rewards of the labor of the negative, must establish a relationship between the knowledge afforded by a university education and the particularities of their diverse selves.

Robert Kegan: Orders of Consciousness

The forms of psychoanalysis that I draw upon most in the following are developmental at their root. But these forms of psychoanalysis are concerned with what development is and how it occurs at the deepest affective levels of the self and the unconscious. Certainly, as a teacher I am concerned with these things too; I want to understand them and how they affect students' learning processes. But as a teacher dealing with young people, I am in no position to change or influence students' deep structures in fundamental ways. At the university level, students appear in my class already formed. But as a teacher, I am able to exert some influence over the areas of cognition or intellection or thinking that appear at relatively surface levels of students' selves.

My difficulty here is that while psychoanalysts have written a great deal about education, they have not written extensively about cognitive or intellectual development. I will in the following, consequently, draw on the work of the educationalist Robert Kegan to provide a more specific account of the developmental move, at the level of intellect and cognition, enjoined of students by the university. I offer this exposition of Kegan's theory not as an assertion of fact but as a heuristic that has allowed me to begin to make more intelligible to myself—and I hope, to others—an outline, at least, of students' developmental move. I do so with full awareness that a theory, especially a strong one—and Kegan's is strong—has the power to shape one's thinking in fundamental ways or to make intelligible things that may not be otherwise. To put it another way, a strong theory, once embraced, has the power to gather unto itself instances that prove it and little power to gather instances that don't.

But Kegan's theory helps me answer, in a different way, a fundamental and simple question. Why do students in the writing class linked with ethics find the study of ethics, in the end, boring and useless, while I, who have attended the same course five times, don't? One reason my students say they find the course boring is that the instructor repeats himself and beats a given point into the ground. Why do students feel this way, when I believe that the instructor has not repeated himself but increasingly examined and deepened his and my apprehension and understanding of a particular argument? The simple answer, according to Kegan, is that I, in the course of my years of education, have moved into what he calls the fourth order of consciousness. My students, though, occupy the third order.

But I should backtrack. Kegan, operating in the tradition of Piaget, Kolhberg, and William Perry, argues that persons may pass through five orders of consciousness in a lifetime. These distinct orders Kegan categorizes, in part, around what he calls different principles of meaning organization. At the first level, roughly ages two to six, children are able to recognize, for example, that objects exist independently of their own sensing of them. At the second level, ages six to the teenage years, children and adolescents "are able to grant objects their own properties irrespective of one's perceptions . . . [and] construct fixed categories and classes into which things can be mentally placed." At the third level, the teenage years and beyond, individuals can "reason abstractly, that is, reason about reason; think hypothetically and deductively" (30).

This last, or third, order of consciousness Kegan associates with traditional societies. In effect, he suggests that within traditional societies, the highest level of development available to the individual was the third order. The possibility of a movement into a fourth order of consciousness is a relatively recent social, political, and historical development. This developmental order exists as a potential for a person to the extent that he or she becomes increasingly situated in modernist institutions. The modern research university, informed by scientific conceptions of knowledge and embracing enlightenment forms of critique, is one such institution.

The developmental movement enjoined of students, frequently in adolescence, by the modernist research university may, according to Kegan, prove a stretch for many. But what precisely is the nature of this stretch? What principle of meaning organization must students master if they are to complete the developmental move into the fourth order? Broadly Kegan suggests that persons at the third level have developed a strong sense of social roles and the responsibilities enjoined by them. They celebrate their own subjectivity and are capable, in empathetic acts, of recognizing the subjectivity of others.

They are not yet positioned, however, to see that these social roles, and the particular subjectivities generated by them, are historically, politically, socially, and institutionally situated. As a consequence, students at the third order cannot "[o]rganize own states or internal parts of self into a systematic whole; distinguish self from one's relationships; see the self as the author (than merely the theater) of one's inner psychological life" (31). The fourth order of consciousness, however, for Kegan represents "a qualitatively more complex system of organizing experience."

It is qualitatively more complex because it takes all of these objects or elements of its system, rather than as the system itself; it does not identify with them but views them as parts of a whole. This new whole is an ideology, an internal identity, a *self-authorship* that can coordinate, integrate, act upon, or invent values, beliefs, convictions, generalizations, ideals, abstractions, interpersonal loyalties, and intrapersonal states. It is no longer *authored by* them, it *authors them* and thereby achieves a personal authority. (185, Kegan's emphasis)

Kegan's suggestive remarks outline a significant and remarkable developmental move at the level of consciousness. The new level of consciousness does not obliterate or wipe out the previous level. One level does not replace the other; rather the fourth level asserts itself as a new principle for the making of meaning, as a reinterpretation of the third. While at the third order, individuals, in celebrating their social roles, also identify with them. And because they identify with them, they take the roles as definitive of the self. As a consequence, the self is experienced as a kind of theater in which things happen.

The movement to the fourth level, consequently, requires that a person somehow break the identifications of the self with its social roles. If this break is accomplished, the self may come to experience itself as something different or distinct from its various social and empirical relations. In effect, at least in its organization of meaning, the self then encompasses its fragmented parts to become the "whole of all there is." At this point, the self ceases to be a theatre in which things happen. Rather, whatever meanings are to be found in events are experienced by the self as self-authored. Through this self-authoring, the self acquires, relative to its knowledge, a degree of personal authority.

This new whole is not the true self or a higher self; it is rather, as Kegan indicates, an "internal identity" and an ideology. This particular ideological self or internal identity is embedded in the very institutional structures and knowledge organization of the modern research university. This is the self that students, who largely occupy the third order of consciousness, must come to understand and to some degree experience if they are to occupy, however momentarily and provisionally, the fourth order of consciousness. When, as teachers of writing, we ask students to write academically, this is the ideology of self that we assert. And when we find students' writing inadequate in this regard, we find most lacking exactly those qualities of the fourth order described by Kegan: the quality of self-authorship (sometimes called "active learning") and the quality of personal authority (sometimes called "voice") that comes with it.

Kant: Representative of the Modernist Order of Consciousness

If I am able to keep Kegan in mind, I can better understand why I still find interest in a course in ethics I have taken five times and my students find boring, having taken it once. Understanding Kant, for example, is not simply a matter of understanding Kant; rather Kant is or is not understood by particular people. The ability of a particular person to understand Kant, as a defining modernist thinker, hinges on whether that person has moved into the fourth order of consciousness as embodied in modernism. That many of my students appear completely flummoxed by Kant means not they do not understand Kant but that they have not yet sufficiently understood the ideology of the modern autonomous self. The attempt to understand Kant, in other words, enjoins of students a developmental move to the extent that Kant's writings exemplify the modernist self.

When I was a student, I did not understand Kant either, but now I can. By this I do not mean that I know Kant in any academic way; I am not an expert on Kant and would not want to argue with anyone about exactly what Kant says. But I do understand him in a basic way because, over the course of my many years of education, I have learned how to assume, however provisionally and momentarily, the fourth order of consciousness. Because I am able to assume the modernist ideological self, I am able to see and understand what Kant says. I experience him as an early manifestation of exactly that modernist self that I have learned to assume.

Kegan's description of the modernist ideology of self seems to me implicit in Kant's moral philosophy, for example. Kant asserts a strict and stern division between the empirical person, who acts out of egoism and desire, and the moral person, who responds to the categorical imperative. This strict division parallels Kegan's description of the fourth order of consciousness as entailing a separation of the self from its relations. Further, as part of the attempt, at least, to act morally in response to the categorical imperative, Kant requires that the individual attempt to universalize any proposed action. This very attempt, even the possibility of it, assumes the autonomy of the individual as that quality that enables the individual to rise to a possible universal position. Finally, Kant argues that one cannot follow a maxim that is self-contradictory. In other words, to will a self-contradictory maxim would mean breaking the internal identify (self equals self) essential to the modernist self.

I am able, then, to understand Kant in a way my students cannot because, having to a degree internalized the modernist ideology of self, I am able to recognize traces of that self in Kant. Once again, I do not say that I know Kant or have knowledge of him. That knowledge belongs to the instructor of the course, to the person immersed in the discipline of ethics. My understanding is not, in other words, shaped by an intellectual grasping of the discipline of ethics but is largely psychologically informed. In Kant, I find a selfobject that affirms narcissistically my self-relation to the modernist ideology of self. It would not be incorrect to say that my understanding of Kant is largely, relative to this particular ideology, empathetic.

I belabor this example of Kant to clarify the dimensions of my simple and fundamental question: why am I able to tolerate (if not quite enjoy) learning about such a figure as Kant for the fifth time when my students, at first exposure, find him utterly befuddling and finally frustrating? It is not because students are not as intelligent as I am, or because they have not read as much, or because they are illiterate. Rather they are exactly where they are supposed to be as young people. They are at the third order of consciousness. They cannot therefore experience Kant as affirming them in their fourth order of consciousness. Instead, before Kant, they experience self-destabilization. Some students even, in the form of a projection, indicate they think Kant is crazy.

The example of Kant, as something frequently taught at universities, may also illustrate the possibility that the central educational mission of the university is to move students to Kegan's fourth order of consciousness. If I assume that to be the case, and if I assume that I, as a teacher of academic writing, am also asking students to make this move, I can begin better to understand why they may have difficulty with academic writing. Learning to master academic writing is not simply a matter of mastering conventions but of actually changing in a basic way one's ideology of self. And if I am able to understand this need for change, I am better positioned to investigate the psychological dimensions of students' developmental moves and explicitly to construct the writing class as a transitional environment.

Postmodernism and the Fifth Order of Consciousness

Kegan posits five possible orders of consciousness. I have not described the fifth. This order, Kegan argues, is a newly emerging one, itself a response to changes in the social, political, and economic world. Roughly, this fifth order is postmodernism. As those familiar with it know, one of the central traits, perhaps the defining characteristic, of postmodernism is and has been its critique of the modernist self. Postmodernism casts into doubt the very idea or possibility of an autonomous self with an internal (self equals self) identity. It suggests that the self is always already situated. Kant's ethic from this perspective is better understood not as a representation of what is but as the rationalization of a particular group or class of people, in Kant's case the rising middle class, or in even broader terms the rationalization of a particularly masculine way of regarding the world (see especially Le Doeuff's reading of Kant as castration complex).

Kegan's description of the modernist self as an ideology suggests that he too participates, to an extent, in the postmodernist perspective and is aware of the postmodernist critique of the modernist self.

But from an educational and developmental perspective, he argues that it makes no sense to teach beginning students, many of whom inhabit the third order of consciousness, the tenets of postmodernism until they have first passed through the fourth order. If, in other words, students have not passed through or learned, however provisionally, to maintain the ideological self of modernism, how will they be able to understand, not just intellectually but empathetically and affectively, the tenets of postmodernism?

Postmodernism and modernism do not present the educator with an either-or situation. Postmodernism does not obliterate or wipe out modernism. Rather postmodernism was implicit in the contradictions and tensions of modernism as ideology. Postmodernism, in moving beyond modernism, represents what Hegel would call a "determinate negation." This negation, as the phrase implies, is not a total or absolute negation of the preceding position but a negation determined in its direction exactly by that which it negates: the modernist self and its implicit and self-generated contradictions and tensions. How is one—or students and teachers, for that matter—to understand postmodernism unless one has understood and passed through modernism? If one has not passed through modernism, one may perhaps learn the conclusions of postmodernism but, having no grasp of how one arrived at those conclusions, will not have been educated into it.

Where does this leave the teacher of writing who works largely with beginning students, most of whom inhabit the third order of consciousness? I believe it leaves them squarely teaching the modernist self. I don't see how one can, without putting students in an untenable position, teach that there is no such thing as an autonomous self. For it is precisely this self that one wants to teach if one wishes also to encourage students to experience the act of writing as a decision-making process. But if there is no autonomous self, there can be no decision maker. If one is spoken by language, and does not speak it, how can one feel responsible for what one has spoken? How can one encourage students to follow Forster's dictum "How do I know what I think until I see what I say" if one puts all those "I's" under erasure?

The suggestion I am making here, that the teaching of post-modernism be put off until students have mastered the fourth level of consciousness, is a strong one and certainly debatable. It may be hard not to teach what is already in one's head. If, in other words, one's principle of meaning organization is postmodernism, how does one keep it out of the picture? I don't know that one can. Indeed, I can't. The forms of psychoanalysis that I use here are themselves postmodern to some degree; these forms argue for the embedded-ness of the self in the social terrain and the potentials in that em-beddedness for fragmentation. The self of psychoanalysis is not autonomous by any stretch of the imagination.

It might appear here that I have fudged. First, I suggest that it is phase appropriate for the instructor of writing to teach students the modernist self. But how is one to do that if, as I have also suggested, it may prove difficult to get the postmodern perspective out of one's head once one has moved to that position? And, indeed, might not some degree of intellectual dishonesty be involved in teaching the modernist self when that very self, from the postmod-ern position, appears false and illusory? How one answers this question would depend on whether one takes it as one's responsibility to teach postmodernism or to teach students. Since I see myself as doing the latter, I don't feel any sense of intellectual dishonesty. Rather, what I have learned of postmodernism and, to a degree, internalized assists me in understanding what students might have to go through, what they may have to experience as they attempt to master the modernist self.

The postmodern critique of the modernist self does not, as I have indicated, wipe out or obliterate by some intellectual fiat the modernist self. It exists and is embodied in actually existing insti-tutions, and until the structures of these institutions change, the modernist self will continue as a functioning and effective ideology of self. This self is embodied in the research university and enjoins of students a developmental move. My awareness of my postmodern position makes it only clearer to me how much I have to work through if I am to arrive at and better understand the subject position of students entering the university, for this position and the modernist position embedded within it necessarily shape and determine my empathetic range.

Related Theoretical Issues

Psychoanalysis and the Conflict Model: Freud and Lacan

Empathy is, as I have argued, a central component in the creation of the writing class as transitional environment. The overall purpose of this environment is to lend students support in making the developmental move entailed by the university.

Kegan writes,

> [I]t is not necessarily a bad thing that adolescents are in over their heads. In fact it may be just what is called for *providing they also experience effective support*. Such supports constitute a holding environment that provides both welcoming acknowledgement of exactly who the person is right now as he or she is, and fosters the person's psychological evolution. As such, a holding environment is a tricky transitional culture, an evolutionary bridge, a context for crossing over. It fosters developmental transformation, or the process of which the whole ("how I am") becomes gradually a part ("how I was") of a new whole ("how I am now"). (43, Kegan's emphasis)

In effect, Kegan describes here what I think the writing class could be, a kind of environment that supports or sustains students in their developmental move. But Kegan's description does not help me to understand what might be involved for students psychologically in such a transition or what might be needed to create an environment that is in fact supportive. Kegan helps me to understand that students at the university are involved in the process of revising their epistemologies or their selves defined as embodiments of a conception of knowledge, what it is, and how it is obtained. But his formulation does not help me to understand why this developmental transition appears to be difficult for so many students. Why, in other words, is the support that Kegan calls for needed at all?

This is a central question and one I consider at length in portions of the following. For the present, I seek to answer this question by means of psychoanalysis as it appears in Heinz Kohut's self psychology and by means of the form of psychoanalysis called *object-relations* as it appears largely in the work of D. W. Winnicott. The work of these psychoanalysts is relatively unknown outside psychoanalytic circles. The question I need immediately to address is why I use the work of these psychoanalysts and not the work of the father of psychoanalysis, Freud, or the work of Lacan, who is much better known to the literary and composition community. This is a question I need to address at some length as a way of suggestion that the work of Kohut and Winnicott is more consonant with the conception of the writing class as transitional environment.

Freud and his true disciple, Lacan, both employ and develop a model of the human psyche that emphasizes the drives. These drives—in Freud's case, sexuality or Eros, and in Lacan's case, desire—impel the individual and bring him or her inevitably into intrapsychic conflict. In Freud, ego is trapped and constantly racked, on the one hand, by the instincts and, on the other, by the irrational demands of the superego, as the internalization of civilization's claims on the individual. In Lacan, desire always exceeds itself, the self loses itself in the social world, and the ego, impelled by desire and unable to locate a resting place, experiences itself as frustration. Moreover, in the theories of both Freud and Lacan, these conflicts appear inherent in the nature of things, in the very structure of the unconscious and its relation to the social order (civilization).

Kohut and Winnicott, while recognizing the psychological experience of conflict, do not argue that it is rooted in the nature of the human animal. Rather they suggest that people may be more or less prone to experience conflict as it arises from an early, relatively good or relatively bad environmental provision. This environment, at the earliest stages, is the mother. Both Winnicott and Kohut argue that the mother's ability to respond to the child physically cannot be separated from the ability of the mother to respond to the child psychologically with empathy. The *way* that the mother feeds the child is as important psychologically as the fact that she feeds the infant is important physically (see especially Winnicott, *Human Nature* 100–15).

In affording the child an optimal psychological provision, the mother assists in helping the child to develop secure self-structures. If, however, the relationship between infant and mother is in some way disturbed, the structures of self shaped by the environment may be relatively weak. If the former is the case, the infant will be able to integrate, with minimal destabilization, the experience of drives (or more precisely being driven, say, by hunger) into its self-structures. If, however, the structures of the self are weak, the infant will not be able to integrate the drive into its structures and will experience itself as being driven. Psychological conflict, then, for both Kohut and Winnicott is not built into the nature of things but arises from disturbance in the early mother-infant dyad.

This difference in attitude toward conflict as something inherent in the nature of things or as arising from a particular and individual disturbed relation to the environment points toward significantly different conceptions of education. As Freud famously remarked, the educator, along with the psychoanalyst and the legislator, all participate in "impossible" professions. These professions are impossible, I believe, because they all participate in and indeed exacerbate the conflict they seek to cure. Educators, psychoanalysts, and legislators are engaged in activities designed to control, redirect, or sublimate the energies of the id. The very activities of civilization, which, as Freud says, advances with a sword in one hand and a bar of soap in the other, produce the conflict. The blood produced with the sword is then cleaned up with the soap, and the conflict between civilization and humanity's animal instincts or drives is potentially endless.

Kohut's and Winnicott's conception of conflict, not as built into the nature of things but as arising from some disturbance in the infant's relation to the environment as mediated through the mother, offers a significantly different conception of education. Education might, from this perspective, be conceived as an extension, however particular, peculiar, and attenuated, of the individual's earliest holding environment. "It," as created and mediated by human beings, might offer students an environment that parallels in its goal and effects the relation of mother to infant. This environment might offer the student not conflict but the opportunity at least for the experience of unity with that environment. The student then, like the infant, through this experience of unity or narcissistic merger, might acquire the support necessary for the restructuring of self, at the levels of cognition and intellection, which are part and parcel of the educational process.

The perspective afforded by Kohut and Winnicott suggests that education is possible. I would say the teaching of writing or, more precisely, the construction of the writing class as transitional environment may serve a powerful educative function. The educative function, however, of writing as the means by which students might master academic writing cannot be separated from the way one conceives of it psychoanalytically. Of writing, Mark Bracher, from his Freudian and Lacanian perspective, writes,

> This psychoanalytic model allows us to see all writing (and all learning, as well) as the product of two basic, conflicting types of intentions, no matter how great the number of specific intentions there might be: first the intention to reinforce and enhance the ego (our dominant sense of self or identity), and second, the intention to express and hence to actualize other, often unconscious identifications, desires, and enjoyments that contradict and thus threaten to destroy the ego's sense of unity and identity. (24–25)

For Bracher, all writing and all learning, for that matter, involve the individual in a basic and primary conflict between the intention to enhance or affirm the ego and the intention to express unconscious desires or identifications. The result of this conflict appears inevitably as a destruction of the ego's unity or identity.

For Bracher, conflict appears to be built into writing. Winnicott

and Kohut offer another possible psychoanalytic model for understanding writing. If we consider writing not as the final product but
as an activity or practice, one may argue that this activity, like bak-
ing, for example, or exercise, may serve a person as a sustaining and
stabilizing selfobject. As I have previously suggested, selfobjects may
function in ways that help people to develop and in ways that don't.
One's selfobject relation to writing may be, in fact, obsessive. The
activity of writing does not, in this instance, serve larger developmental purposes but acts defensively to ward off feelings of interior
disintegration, emptiness, and purposelessness. But in either case,
whether as serving developmental or defensive ends, writing does
not necessarily produce conflict and a weakening of the ego but has
the potential at least to produce self-stability and intactness.

If this kind of writing is the case, then in the creation of the
writing class as transitional environment, the activity of writing may
be understood and presented as, potentially at least, a selfobject. As
such, this activity would not necessarily entail the subjective experience of conflict but would offer the possibility, however momentarily, of self-stabilization. Remember, I am speaking here of writing as an activity, as something that occurs in time and space. That
one may experience the activity as stabilizing does not mean the
writing as product, as finished or published, might not appear rife
with contractions, tensions, and conflicts. But these signs of conflict I take, especially in students' work, not as a sign that writing
necessarily involves conflict but as a sign that the student has not
been able to experience the activity of writing as self-stabilizing or
momentarily restorative. And, indeed, at times, I have experienced
the conflicts I have noted in student writing, especially if the student appears at least partly aware of the conflict, not as a sign that
the student is in conflict but as an indication that the conflict may
stabilize the student against fragmentation.

I hope I have made clear that the difference I have traced between the post-Freudian and the Freudian conceptions of the psyche
does not represent merely a squabble within psychoanalysis. Rather,
I side with and use the post-Freudians because their view of the
psyche makes possible a different conception of writing classroom

and its purposes. If one takes the view of the post-Freudians, one may begin to conceive of the writing class as a kind of environment that might support students in their developmental move. In addition, one may conceive of writing in a different way, not as symbolic representation of students' intrapsychic conflicts but as an activity that may stabilize or restore students during the necessary destabilization that attends development.

Kohut: Empathy and Narcissism

In *Persons in Process: Four Stories of Writing and Personal Development in College,* Marcia Curtis, in addition to supplying an excellent overview of Kohut, writes evocatively of her first encounter with his work and the ways that it helped her better to understand her role as teacher and researcher. In outlining the implications of Kohut's notion of empathy for teaching, she writes,

> Empathy requires the more complex, honest act of truly listening for the meanings behind our students' written and oral expressions in order to convey a true understanding— an understanding that recognizes when to mirror their successes along with their struggles, when to offer the idealizing force explicit instruction can supply, when to acknowledge the alienating as well as sustaining powers held by new and old discourse communities. It requires, in essence, modulating our instructional response to our students' personal and educational needs rather than according to our own personal, theoretical or institutional desires. (Harrington and Curtis 31)

In this passage, Curtis affords a vision of the writing classroom as what I call a transitional environment. I wholly embrace this vision, but while Curtis does great justice to the role of empathy in the construction of such an environment, she does not in these remarks and in her general exposition of Kohut emphasize his other significant contribution to the psychoanalytic tradition: his development of the concept of narcissism. In the following, I offer a brief but slightly more technical exposition of that concept.

The primary text for an understanding of the concept and its later development in the psychoanalytic tradition is Freud's "On Narcissism: An Introduction." There Freud points to something he had not hitherto noticed, and that is a form of narcissism that does not represent a perversion but that may be "the libidinal component to the egoism of the instinct of self-preservation, a measure of which may justifiably be attributed to every living creature" (18). This form of narcissism Freud calls "primary" and finds its most apparent manifestation in children, most especially in "His Majesty the Baby." "Secondary narcissism" may be observed in the adult. Freud writes,

> We should then say: the sick man withdraws his libidinal cathexes back upon his own ego, and sends them out again when he recovers. "Concentrated is his soul," says Wilhelm Busch of the poet suffering from toothache, "in his molar's narrow hole." (25)

In moments of organic suffering, secondary narcissism appears for Freud as a withdrawal of libidinal cathexes from the individual's normal objects and a concentration of it wholly within the individual's ego.

Freud summarizes:

> A person may love
> (1) according to the narcissistic type
>   (a) what he himself is (i.e., himself)
>   (b) what he himself was
>   (c) what he himself would like to be
>   (d) someone who was once part of himself
> (2) according to the anaclitic (attachment) type
>   (a) the woman who feeds him
>   (b) the man who protects him
> and the succession of substitutes who take their place. (33)

While Freud's attitude toward narcissism is one of scientific impartiality, his association of narcissism with perversions (in which Freud includes homosexuality), infants, and beautiful women leaves the distinct impression that the form of object relating true of the narcissistic type is inferior to that of the "anaclitic" type. Of beautiful women, for example, Freud writes, "[S]trictly speaking, it is only themselves that such women love" (31). Much is implied in that *only*.

Kohut's single greatest contribution to psychoanalytic theory lies in his reevaluation of the concept of narcissism. And, in my opinion, had Kohut not worked through this concept, it is doubtful he would have been led to his fruitful insights on the role and importance of empathy in psychological development. In *Theories of Object Relations: Bridges to Self-Psychology*, Bascal and Newman write,

> Kohut "de-moralized" the concept of "narcissistic" needs by asserting that they are distortions of essentially healthy, that is, developmentally legitimate, *selfobject* needs, and that they emerge as a result of the rupture of essential *selfobject* relationships. Kohut's re-conceptualization of selfobject relationships as those in which the object-world is experienced as providing a diversity of sustaining functions throughout life was revolutionary. (12–13)

Certainly, as the authors assert, Kohut did seek quite explicitly to demoralize the concept of narcissism and to free it from the association, clearly found in Freud, with moral notions of self-absorption, egocentricity, or simple selfishness. More important, this reevaluation of the concept led Kohut to an entirely different formulation of the role of narcissism in psychological life. People have, he asserts, selfobject or narcissistic needs. The ability, moreover, to establish narcissistically satisfying relations to selfobjects is essential to the stability of the self.

As Bascal and Newman argue, Kohut's reevaluation of the concept allows for a reinterpretation of those forms of narcissism more associated with self-centeredness or selfishness, not as a condemnation of the human need for sustaining selfobjects but as indications of disruptions or disturbances in an individual's narcissistically sustained relation to its self objects. From this perspective, it is possible to read the narcissism Freud located in beautiful women, who can love *only* themselves, in a different way. In effect, the self-containment Freud locates in beautiful women may be read not as a direct expression of primary or grandiose narcissism but as a form of defense or self-protection. The woman of great beauty may withdraw into herself not because she is egocentric or incapable of object relating but because of the potentials particular to being a woman of great beauty for narcissistic wounding. The narcissism, then, of the woman of great beauty may not represent a form of perverted object relations but may be an expression of a healthy narcissism that says, in effect, "I am more than beauty" or "My relations to the world are more diverse and more complex than can ever be expressed in the single relation of my beauty."

The pedagogical implications of this conception of narcissism, for education in general and for the teacher of writing in particular, are several. First, it allows me to understand the seeming inability of some students to relinquish in writing their egocentric views of the world, as rooted in unquestioned personal belief and personal experience, as expressions, possibly at least, of healthy narcissism. This apparent inability may not represent a cognitive deficiency or an unwillingness to think. Instead the apparent narcissism (in the pejorative sense) of students' responses may represent their attempts to maintain a degree of self-stability in the face of ways of thinking and conceptions of knowledge that disturb, in more unconscious ways, their relationships to their intellectual selfobjects. In turn, this apparent narcissism suggests that the developmental move enjoined by the university (as a movement to Kegan's forth order of consciousness) is in fact working. Students have or are in the process of experiencing, at relatively unconscious levels, various forms of destabilization and narcissistic wounding as they experience the implications of the university's particular epistemology for their own ways of knowing.

Kohut's conception of narcissism further allows for a conception of education as serving a developmental function. As a prelude to what I mean by this, I think of R. D. Laing's "Peter." Peter, Laing notes, showing signs of anxiety, had to withdraw from a group discussion. When Laing asked why, Peter said, "They are just arguing but I am arguing for my life." Given the fragility of his self—Peter was a schizophrenic—Peter experienced a questioning of his particular beliefs as an assault upon his sense of self. He had to withdraw because he experienced fragmentation. The writings of students too, within the social environs of the university, may be, in some instances, arguments for their very selves. Given that the selves of our students are essentially more stable than Peter, students are not likely to experience the challenges to their beliefs as productive of panic-stricken retreat. To put the matter another way, those who Peter saw as just arguing may have been indeed arguing for their very selves but the nature of their relationship to their beliefs did not lead them to experience a challenge to those beliefs as self-fragmentation on the order of that experienced by Peter.

The developmental function that exposure to the ways of knowing implicit in the institutional structures of the university imparts may then be best conceived not as an attempt to change student's beliefs, to show them that their beliefs are wrong, but to influence the ways that they psychologically hold these beliefs and the conceptions of knowledge implicit in them. While Kohut's psychology is developmental, he does not, unfortunately, detail the changes in narcissistic need that may occur as the individual moves from infancy to childhood, to adolescence and beyond. But clearly adolescence—which I am prepared to argue now extends well into a person's twenties, especially in the middle class—is a time when young people, as Winnicott argues, are concerned with their beliefs, do begin to question authority and to negotiate an altered relation to their beliefs. The university education participates in this developmental move and imparts to it a particular direction.

I believe this direction, if achieved, may be profoundly significant in the development of the individual. He or she may come to retain or hold his or her beliefs with a relatively greater flexibility and less endangerment to the self. One might come to a greater tolerance for the narcissistic wounding inherent in the questioning of one's belief. With this increased tolerance, one might then be positioned to examine one's beliefs *as one's beliefs* and not as affording one epistemological access to an implacable and unchanging reality. Again, this examination would mean not trying to change students' beliefs but assisting them in developing an altered relationship to those beliefs. This is no small or easy matter.

But while Kohut does not detail in a precise way the different developmental stages of the individual's narcissistic needs, he does suggest, in "Forms and Transformations of Narcissism," that narcissism, the very stuff of the self's relation to its object, may alter in positive and healthful ways. He notes, as indications of this change, an increased capacity for empathy, increased creative engagement with one's daily activities, a sense of humor, and finally wisdom. Expressed in this way, Kohut's characterization of the most highly developed forms of narcissism appears downright banal. What is not banal, however, is his claim that the qualities do not arise from the ability to reason more clearly about one's experience, or to be objective, or to have adopted realistic values, but from a transformation in narcissism. He writes,

> I believe this rare feat [the capacity to recognize one's transience] rests not simply on a victory of autonomous reason and supreme objectivity over the claims of narcissism, but on the creation of a higher form of narcissism. (81)

Clearly, in this relatively early writing, Kohut does acknowledge that autonomous reason and supreme objectivity may play a significant role in "the creation of a higher form of narcissism." Later, however, especially in his ongoing analysis of Freud, he shifts his analysis in significant ways. Truth and the pursuit of it, through rationality and objectivity, come to represent Freud's narcissistically sustained commitment to a particular set of values. This set of values may have functioned for Freud in psychologically healthful ways, and they may so function also for other people, but they by no means represent the full range of values that might lead to a transformation of narcissism.

Universities still, to some degree, represent repositories of the products of autonomous reason and supreme objectivity. Certainly, pedagogically, they attempt to present themselves that way. And among the great body of students, there may be some who already vibrate with the Ideal, the pursuit of truth that universities represent. These students may be sustained in the ups and downs of their education by the pursuit of precisely this idea. I believe myself to have been once such student. The university, for its part, through its elaborate forms of apprenticeship, seeks to locate and encourage just such persons as a way of perpetuating its own institutional structures and the ideal it purports to represent. For these relatively few students, a university education might be said to work, not because it has done its job in any way effectively but because the individual student, sustained by of his or her narcissistically infused ideal, has made it work.

We cannot anticipate then that simply because we hold up or seek to embody the pursuit of truth, students will find themselves narcissistically reflected and fueled by that ideal. The great bulk of students will not devote themselves to the pursuit of truth as their sustaining ideal. But we can expect that the university's embodiment of this ideal in its formulation of disciplines, methodologies, and general epistemology will effect students' sense of selves and might, as I argue, assist in the transformation of narcissism from relatively archaic to relatively more mature forms at the level of intellection. Kohut writes,

> In the progression from information through knowledge to wisdom, the first two can still be defined almost exclusively within the sphere of cognition itself. The term information refers to the gleaning of isolated data about the world; knowledge is the comprehension of a cohesive set of such data held together by a matrix of abstractions. Wisdom, however, goes beyond the cognitive sphere, although of course, it includes it. (83)

This passage makes two important points. First, the pursuit of the ideal of truth is not exclusively allied with the transformation of narcissism as it appears in wisdom. Second, while wisdom is not reducible either to information or to knowledge, a passage through the sphere of knowledge appears integral to a transformation of narcissism as it appears in the personal quality of wisdom.

The success of the university in assisting students in their development may be better measured not by the university's capacity to garner recruits to the ideal of truth but by its ability to engage students in the world of knowledge as an integral step toward wisdom. Wisdom is not an abstraction, nor is it knowledge of things or a capacity to think abstractly. It has something much more to do with the knowledge required for daily living and ultimately, if only momentarily attained, as an experience of the self in a stabilizing and sustaining relation to its objects. What if students seek in their university educations not knowledge per se, or methodologies, or systems of thought, but the self-staining and guiding wisdom that might accrue from a passage through knowledge? If this is the case, then the ultimate pedagogical function of the university might be to present knowledge not under the aegis of the pursuit of truth but as a means by which wisdom may be achieved.

Viewed in this light and relative to an overall course of development, the university environment and its particular conceptions of knowledge may prove destabilizing for students not so much because it casts into doubt their particular beliefs as epistemological claims but because the university plunges the student, at the level of ideation, into to the realm of transience and contingency. Kohut writes,

> Wisdom is largely achieved though man's ability to overcome his unmodified narcissism and it rests on his acceptance of the limitations of his physical, intellectual, and emotional powers. It may be defined as an amalgamation of the higher processes of cognition with the psychological attitude which accompanies the renouncement of these narcissistic demands. (83)

The acceptance of limitations, Kohut suggests in another place, may also be described as the acceptance of one's finitude, and the capacity to experience oneself, however momentarily, sub specie aeternitatis. But this acceptance, if truly allied to wisdom, means not a retreat from the world but rather a continued and relatively stable narcissistic relation to it and to one's particular ideals.

Clearly, Kohut here defines wisdom in relation to the capacity of the individual to face the prospect of his or her death with relative tranquility. Facing the prospect of one's death is not, however, a developmental necessity for the young. Wisdom, Kohut argues, in its fullest dimensions is more likely to arrive later in life. Still, I argue that the epistemology of the university does require students to face not precisely their deaths but the contingency and the historicity of their beliefs. The ability to master theory may not require the ability to see one's life sub specie aeternitatis, but it may well require the student to view his or her life sub specie "sociologicus" or "philosophocus" or "empiricisticus." What the student must do, relative to these theories, is emotionally complex and trying. The student must be positioned to view his or her own life as an alien might view it while, with a relative calm, still maintaining a highly charged narcissistic allegiance to that life in all its detail and complexity. Indeed, students must accomplish this difficult task if they are to pass through the sphere of knowledge in ways that may lead to a transformation of narcissism.

Sadly, the great bulk of students do not reap the rewards of psychological development that might attend a university education. The step from self as narcissistically embedded in its sustaining objects to a view of that self as, for example, sub species ethicus is too great, not because the step is too great but because the need for such a step is not recognized or supported institutionally. And because this step is not recognized and institutionally supported, students too frequently abandon the effort.

Feminism and the Modernist Self

The relationship of psychoanalysis, in a general way, to social and political movements has not always been happy. Certain variants of psychoanalysis appear, to put the matter flatly, completely to ignore issues of race, gender, and class. Instead, psychoanalysis valorizes the individual and thus tacitly supports ideologies of individualism. A great deal, however, depends on what one means by "individual." The forms of psychoanalysis I employ here stress that, in fact, there is no such thing as the isolated individual. Individuals rather exist only as they are sustained by and through their object or self-relations to objects. And central to the identities of individuals are their relationships to class, gender, and race.

I locate in feminism much that seems to support a psychoanalytic perspective on the pedagogical process. I value especially the feminist critique of the ways of knowing of the university as implicated in structures of domination. Still, I understand that my assertion of the importance of the modernist self for development may appear to put my psychological perspective at odds with feminism. To be clear, what I wish to preserve of the modernist self is the potential in it for bringing students to what I call the extrospective moment, a moment I believe that goes hand in hand with notions of self-consciousness and self-reflexivity. What I critique is the way the university teaches this developmental moment. It does it monolithically and with no recognition of the trials and tribulations involved for students in moving to this moment.

Feminism affords an analysis of why this poor method of teaching something so important might be the norm. The university as an institutionalized and socially supported representation of the modernist self may serve primarily as a vehicle of domination. The reason it cannot recognize the selves of individuals is simple. It is a pedagogy of power; its purpose, far from developmental or educational in the sense that I mean the terms, may be to further socialize people into the already existing power imbalance between men and women.

This possibility is clearly implied, for example, in Carol Gilligan's *In a Different Voice*. Gilligan argues that men and women follow different developmental paths; the former are bent on separation from the mother, while the latter feel no such need. The result, overall, is that men and women come to possess different notions of morality, with the additional significant difference that the moral position of men is institutionally and socially recognized and sustained and that of women is not. Gilligan writes,

> The elusive mystery of women's development lies in its recognition of the continuing importance of attachment in the human life cycle. Woman's place in man's life cycle is to protect this recognition while the developmental litany intones the celebration of separation, autonomy and natural rights. (23)

The developmental litany to which Gilligan refers are theories of development produced by men on the basis of studies that quite amazingly, in some instances, did not include women at all. There is more than a gross parallel between the developmental cycle based on men—one that leads to separation, individuation, and autonomy—and the "modernist" epistemological self that informs the pedagogy of the university. The blindness of the former to the experience of women as possibly different from that of men may well be related to the blindness of the latter relative to the experiences that both men and women undergo upon entry to the university.

For example, the Kantian ethic appears to be a prototypical representation of the modernist (and male) self. Kant stresses, throughout his work, rights and the ability to rise to autonomy as things somehow distinct from the contingent self, the self attached to the world and motivated by desire. This ethic stands in stark contrast to an ethics of attachment. For example, in *Ethical Insights: A Brief Introduction*, Douglas Birsch uses a chart to classify diverse ethical theories in relation to three assumptions of traditional ethics. These assumptions, phrased as questions, are

> Is ethics rational?
> Are people moral agents?
> Can we universalize some ethical evaluations?

According to the author of this text, the answer of Kantian ethics to each of these questions is "yes." The answer, however, of an ethics of care, as explicated by the author on the work largely of Nell Noddings, to each of these questions is "no" (125).

These *yes's* and *no's* suggest rather starkly the distinction between a view of ethics based on notions of autonomy and individuation and a notion of ethics, as found in Noddings, based on attachment and caring. Indeed, one may note more than a difference. In light of the traditional assumptions of ethics, while Kant fits the bill entirely, Noddings's ethics does not at all. In short, so profound are the differences that an ethics of caring does not seem to qualify, from the perspective of traditional ethics, as an ethics at all. It is not enough to say that traditional ethics and the ethics of caring represent incommensurable forms of discourse. Rather, given the power imbalance between these ethical perspectives, the assumptions of traditional ethics blind it to the assumptions of an ethics of caring.

Painted in this way, the modernist self appears an ideological representation which serves and perpetuates a power imbalance that regulates an ethics of attachment and caring to the realm of the impenetrable other. Given, then, that the forms of psychoanalysis I employ here are very much theories of attachment, what possible value may be located in the modernist self? The value for students in the modernist self is purely a developmental one. I in no way posit the modernist self as a final repository of knowledge or as the ultimate stage of development. It is not gold to be hoarded. Rather its value lies wholly in what it might bring about developmentally.

What this development might be is a revised psychological relation, for the self, to the subject-object division. Before the developmental move is made, a person may be inclined to experience the subject-object division as fixed, at the levels of intellection and cognition, in reality. From this position, one says, with some pride, I am me and you are not. The capacity to make this distinction between self and nonself is the hard-won product of a highly complex psychological development. But this position, once achieved, is fraught with perils for further development. What if the "I" in this instance is male and the "you" is female. If this is the case, the person's participation in modernist institutions and its epistemology may lead to the participation of that person in structures of domination. And if that is the case, the person may, in light of the existing power imbalance that presents itself in the surrounding social terrain, come to experience his or her position in the structures of domination as narcissistically sustaining. At this juncture, one might say, with some pride, "I am superior and more powerful and you are not."

These remarks suggest the powerful appeal of the modernist autonomous self and the ways a person's identification with this position may perpetuate existing power relations. But in the work of the psychoanalyst and feminist Jessica Benjamin, one may begin to locate at least a theoretical way out of the impasse of the power imbalance, within the confines of the analytic situation and, I believe, to some degree within the pedagogical one. She writes,

> As psychoanalysis moves from its original subject-object paradigm to an intersubjectivity one, we subtly change the meaning of activity; we conceive it in the context not of a polar complementarity but of symmetry between two active partners. And this allows a reconfiguration of terms. However uncertain their contents, masculinity and femininity are no longer in the same formal relation to each other, separated by an uncrossable, fixed divide. Within the subject-object paradigm, there is always one subject, never two, it is necessary that whatever one side gains the other must lose. In that formal structure the Other, let us say woman, could only become subject by reversal, by displacing man into the position of object, which would hardly have been acceptable. In a sense, the idea of subjectivity could not be extended to woman within the subject-object paradigm because only reversal, not extension of the subject-object position was possible. In that construction, activity had to be subtracted from femininity or inevitably passivity would devolve onto the masculine. (39–40)

In summary, Benjamin argues that the subject-object division, as it appears especially in the empiricism of Freud, embodies a power relationship relative to the sexes. If men, in other words, conceived of themselves or in praxis experience themselves as subjects, women necessarily become objects. Two important conclusions may be derived from this. First, in relation to the formal subject-object division, men and women are "separated by an uncrossable, fixed divide," and women necessarily are reduced to object status and deprived of subjectivity.

But Benjamin also suggests a way out of this dilemma. She argues that, in effect, in Freud and in empiricism generally, the subject-object division rested on a deeper and relatively unexamined activity-passivity dialectic. The subject, in other words, is identified with the former and the object with the latter. But she argues, as psychoanalysis moves from the subject-object division to a notion of intersubjectivity, the notion of action may be subtly redefined. Benjamin does not throw out the subject-object division but instead suggests a redefinition of it. It remains, relative to a redefinition of activity, as symmetry between two active partners.

These ruminations are abstruse but important in affording an understanding of the developmental value I locate in learning the subject-object division. To illustrate, where Benjamin writes, "let us say women," instead let us substitute, "let us say students." From this perspective, the subject-object division appears not an epistemological distinction as much as the epistemological component (or rationalization) of a power relationship. Teachers are cast as the subject (active and possessed of subjectivity), and students are cast as objects (passive and lacking in subjectivity). Some anecdotal evidence that this casting may actually be the case may be located in frequent instructor laments that students are passive, unengaged, and unwilling to exercise their own initiative.

This casting may appear a repetition, albeit in a more elusive vocabulary, of Friere's banking model, in which students appear to be empty vessels into which knowledge is stuffed. Certainly, Friere's metaphor describes in a stark way the power relationship between student and teacher, but it does not do justice to the psychological reality either of the teacher or of the student. Following Benjamin into the realm of the intersubjective, I suggest that for students, being or becoming passive is a kind of activity. Students, in other words, do have subjectivities, and becoming passive before the knowledge they are afforded is a highly complex form of psychological activity. Too frequently, this activity amounts to the student, having experienced narcissistic wounding, simply withdrawing his or her narcissism from the object of study. If, however, the achievement of this passivity were recognized as involving a complex psychological process, one may locate in the educational process the potential at least for students to take up the subject-object distinction as a psychological process, not to locate a final reality but to negotiate the me and the not-me.

In summary, the feminist perspective offers a telling critique of the autonomous self and its ideological role in maintaining and forwarding current power relations. But the work of Benjamin, at least, offers a reconceptualization of the subject-object division that might allow instructors of writing to use the currently existing power relationship toward developmental rather than ideological ends. I do not wish to minimize the difficulties implicit in the implementation of such pedagogy within the context of existing power relationships. But because my perspective is resolutely psychoanalytic, I believe, in light of concerns raised by gender and class studies, that an approach of the kind I recommend is all the more urgent. I agree, in other words, with Winnicott, who argues, that people will go no farther in creating new social and political relationships than they can go in their psychological development.

2 / Academic Writing, Destabilization, and Extrospection

If the purpose of the writing class as transitional environment is to assist students in making the developmental move enjoined by the university, then the writing class should have a content—a set of readings particularly—that could be defined as academic. I will have more to say about what I think academic writing is from a psychological point of view. For the present, I will avoid any attempt at defining *academic readings and writings* by referring instead to the broader context of the situation: the university, which produces them. I read, somewhere, that universities may be regarded as places where generalizations are generated.

This is a snappy if somewhat sloppy definition. Generalizations are generated everywhere and may be generated also by racists intent on the production of Internet propaganda. But I still find the definition at least moderately usable because one complaint students have registered with great regularity about the readings I have assigned is that they "generalize," "overgeneralize," and are "extreme." These are very peculiar complaints. I do not think I am naïve in believing that the great bulk of my students would not say that racist propaganda "overgeneralizes." They would say it is "wrong." When students criticize something as an "overgeneralization," they are registering an epistemological, not a moral, complaint.

I take this odd complaint as a sign that students have begun to enter into a psychological or self-relationship to the epistemology of the university. Irene Papoulis writes, "As a university writing teacher, I am dismayed by the infectiousness of the notion that to think well in a discipline one must put aside one's subjective reactions to academic material" (133). I am dismayed too, since these subjective reactions seem to me integral to the developmental move students are undertaking. I want such subjective reactions, and for this reason, some academic materials—of the kind that may elicit complaints of "overgeneralization"—are necessary.

In one particular reading-and-writing unit I taught, the topic was biodiversity. I realized afterward that the assignment was a mistake, for me and for my students, and the psychological or subjective responses that might have been produced by a topic like biodiversity are examined in this chapter. The way I had students write on this topic—a summary—may have blinded me to the possible psychological repercussions of the assignment. My approach was, perforce, craft-oriented, and following Wendy Bishop, I will examine the ways this approach to the teaching of writing constructs the intersubjectivity of the writing class.

Through an analysis of several students' writing on the topic of biodiversity, I came to more firmly believe that the move to self-authorship may require a significant revision in students' relationships to language and how they experience it. Students must move from a notion of language as embedded in the world of common sense, as expressive primarily of a unity with others of a particular social group, toward a notion of the word as concept. Inherent in this move is the potential for a double destabilization. I went through the same experience as I attempted to understand what was meant by the Russian Revolution.

A Unit: Academic Writing on Biodiversity

The course for which I designed the unit involving biodiversity is taken primarily by students in their first year at the university and is the single course required of all students. Its official label is Writing 2. I work in a program with an emphasis on writing across the curriculum, and Writing 2 has been designed to reflect that emphasis. It is divided into three units: science, social science, and the humanities. The first unit, on science, was an ongoing bone of contention. I, given my understanding of the university as a modernist institution inculcated with the epistemological ideal of science, believed such a unit might serve developmental purposes.

I don't believe, however, that I would have devised the unit on biodiversity had I not, at the time, been in charge of the training and supervision of some fifteen teaching assistants who would be teaching Writing 2 for the first time. I knew that the teaching assistants, largely drawn from departments in the humanities, were least comfortable with the science unit. I did not have to ask to find this out, since teaching assistants freely expressed their reservations about the unit. I saw their point and sought out a topic that I hoped might not utterly undermine their confidence as they stepped out of their particular disciplines and into the writing classroom for the first time.

Biodiversity recommended itself. I already knew a little about it, having taught a number of research writing courses for students drawn entirely from the introductory sequence in biology. And because of that work, I was able to lay my hands on articles written by scientists for the generally informed and college-educated public. But while they were written for the general public, the articles were full of charts and graphs and were information-laden. Strange things like "diatoms" were mentioned. I felt, though, that the scientists were writing on an important subject, one having to do with the fate of the ecosystem, and that the articles offered examples of how scientists wrote and how they establish their authority.

I thought the topic might work. Since all of the teaching assistants would be teaching the same unit, I hoped they might help each other. I also decided—and this was a critical step—and asserted that teaching assistants should use the topic of biodiversity to teach students more about how to write summary. I had three principal reasons for doing this. First, I hoped that whatever their misapprehensions about the topic of biodiversity, the teaching assistants might get a handle on the unit through the teaching of summary. It is a fairly restricted form and lent itself, I thought, to the scientific materials. Second, I felt that having students write summary might rule out of bounds other forms of students' responses. I wanted students actually to read the articles and to pay attention to the information offered and how it was offered. I did not want the articles to serve as a pretext for largely opinionated arguments about whether or not the world was or wasn't going, ecologically speaking, to hell in a handbasket.

Finally, I felt that offering some instruction in summary to students might serve them well in their other courses, especially those in general education. As part of my work with "linked" writing courses, I have over the years attended many general education courses. All of them had been laden with information, and when students had to write either a short paper or essay midterms and finals, they wrote mostly summary. Indeed, when a student for such a course asked the instructor what they should write for an upcoming paper, he answered, "Well, it's 80 percent summary and like 20 percent your own thoughts, you know."

But while I believe I thought the assignment through clearly in relation to the needs both of students and of teaching assistants, I must report that the results I received from my own teaching of this unit were not as I had hoped. Mostly I received just summary with little or none of that magical 20 percent mixed in. Indeed, at an extreme, students' work was sometimes so fragmented and incoherent that I would have to stop reading a paper midway through. I simply could not go on. Indeed, relative to what I was reading, there was no path, no way to go on. And if I looked inside myself at these moments, it seemed that all the student wanted to do was to get the experience of writing this particular paper over with as soon as possible. Students clearly did not experience the activity of writing in this instance as self-stabilizing; instead, it seemed that before my eyes, students' selves disintegrated into fragmentation and panic.

Destabilization: The Strangeness of Science

If what I felt was not a projection—and I don't believe it was—I must ask why? Why should writing a summary on a topic like biodiversity produce for students the experience of self-fragmentation? I can perhaps begin to answer this question through introspection and putting myself in students' shoes. Before I started reading on the subject, I did not know that scientists have managed to catalogue only about 1.4 million species and that they don't even know how many species there really are. I didn't know what a cichlid was: a family of perchlike fish that may comprise 5 percent (an impressive number) of all vertebrate species. Nor have I, to my knowledge, directly experienced any of the loss of biodiversity that many scientists argue is occurring. If anything, when at the grocery store, I experience an expanded variety of species coming in from all over the world. I had never eaten a mango until about three years ago. When a bird that once shared my environment is gone, I simply assume it has gone someplace else.

These reflections point in several directions, but they add up to one pregnant thought: I know next to nothing about the material or natural world that sustains me and my kind in our being. But even to be able to arrive at this thought requires an acceptance of the claim of science to represent or assert knowledge. This acceptance is itself no small thing and represents one of the central elements involved in that epistemological revision necessary to move to the fourth order of consciousness. Much of what science tells us is counterintuitive and contradicts those ordinary, daily sense certainties that constitute our shared and sharable human reality.

Kegan does not make this particular analogy, but I believe that what he calls third-order consciousness is rooted in the sense certainty of daily life and in the common sense generated by an assumption of shared sense certainty. A classic instance for me of the intertwining of sense certainty and common sense, as a directive for how one should act, is the saying, "You do not have to hit yourself over the head with a hammer to know that it hurts." This saying is itself a bit of common sense in the form of a dictum or rule of thumb. It seems, moreover, to be telling the truth because it is rooted in the sense certainty that hitting oneself on the head with a hammer would hurt. This is the reality of everyday life. It is not the reality of Macbeth, who in a nearly delusional state, might ask—and I paraphrase—"Is this I a hammer I see before me or just a hammer of the mind?"

Destabilization: The Challenge of Science to Common Sense

Arriving at the fourth order of consciousness requires an uprooting of the self from its narcissistically informed conceptions, beliefs, ideas, thoughts, and intuitions, what Kegan would call "durable categories." These categories are considered durable because they are rooted in shared or common sense. Some substantiation for and clarification of this claim appear in the following, by Berger and Luckman from their *Social Construction of Reality:*

> The reality of everyday life is taken for granted *as* reality. It does not require additional verification over and beyond its simple presence. It is simply *there* as self-evident and compelling facticity. I *know* that it is real. While I am capable of engaging in doubt about its reality, I am obliged to suspend such doubt as I routinely exist in everyday life. This suspension of doubt is so firm that to abandon it, as I might want to do, say, in theoretical or religious contemplation, I have to make an extreme transition. (23, Berger's emphasis)

Berger and Luckman's description of the reality of everyday life as taken for "granted as reality" seems self-evidently true. In normal daily life, I must take this reality for granted as the grounds of my very possibility of activity. I may doubt this reality occasionally, but I rarely do, unless I am delusional. The capacity, then, to sustain doubt about this reality for the sake of theoretical or religious contemplation requires, as Berger and Luckman indicate, that the individual undergo an *extreme transition.*

This transition is implicit in the move from third- to fourth-order consciousness and may be experienced as extreme by the person who is enjoined to make the move. One reason this move may be experienced as extreme I have already suggested. Initially, the move may be experienced as a transition from reality into subjective delusion. And if one is able to maintain the theoretical position, one may experience oneself as objective and the shared reality of everyday life as mass delusion. This view too might be experienced as extreme. Berger and Luckman write,

> The reality of everyday life further presents itself to me as an intersubjective world, a world I share with others. This intersubjectivity sharply differentiates everyday life from other realities of which I am conscious. I am alone in the world of my dreams, but I know that the world of everyday life is as real to others as it is to myself. . . . I also know of course that the others have a perspective on this common world that is not identical with mine. My "here" is their "there." My "now" does not overlap with theirs. My projects differ from and may even conflict with theirs. All the same, I know that I live with them in a common world. (23)

From a certain theoretical or moral perspective, it might not be common sense at all to have cars and freeways. But when I am in my car and on the freeway, I very much rely upon, as the basis of this activity, a shared and intersubjective commonsense world. If my fellow human beings were to lose their sense certainty and to begin to doubt the very existence of those white lines on the freeway that regulate the comportment of all, I could be in real trouble. Indeed, even though I may not be immediately threatened, I may feel anger at someone who does not appear to recognize our shared and intersubjective world but, apparently off in his own world, following his own rules, drives in a way that endangers others.

As Kegan suggests, the movement into autonomy and self-authorship requires that one no longer see the self as its relations to the world. But if Luckman and Berger are right, the self, as rooted in what they call natural consciousness, defines itself in a most elemental way through a relation of intersubjectivity. I assume, indeed I know, that the other inhabits the same natural consciousness I do. Thus our world is "inter" or shared, but at the same time, on the basis of this sharing, I also know that the other has his or her own subjectivity, that his or her goals are not necessarily the same as mine. When an ambulance races by, I do not necessarily feel the driver is driving recklessly; I assume instead that the driver shares my reality but has a different (subjective) goal or project.

Self-Destabilization

These reflections might seem to take us rather far from the simple question, "Why did my students write such poor summaries on the topic of biodiversity?" Would not a simpler explanation be that many of the students who wrote poor summaries have poor writing skills? This answer seems to me, however, something of a circular explanation. The students I teach are drawn from the top 12 percent of all students in the state. It is clear they have acquired a certain level of skill as writers; otherwise they would not be in my class. Certainly they should be able to build on these skills to write a summary, in some ways, at least, one of the least difficult forms of writing. I argue, however, that students cannot build on skills previously acquired precisely because those skills are rooted in third-order consciousness.

As the above reflections on common sense and intersubjectivity are intended to suggest, students' confrontation with a scientific topic like biodiversity may produce a degree of destabilization not only in their epistemologies but also in their very experience of their self-relation to the world. While common sense and everyday life are experienced as intersubjective or ultimately human, the facts offered by science contradict common sense and reveal a "world" indifferent to human intentions. Science is not intersubjective, nor is the relation of the individual to the facts and claims of science. The relation that informs scientific knowledge is that of subject to object; it is an epistemological relationship.

The topic of biodiversity brings with it a particular and peculiar potential for destabilization in addition to the self-destabilization inherent in a confrontation with science. Indeed, when I asked students to write summaries of articles about biodiversity, I was aware of this potential destabilization and hoped that I might, by insisting on summary, rule it out of bounds. Clearly, though, the potential for this destabilization—whether students wrote about it or not—was present, for while the articles I assigned were information-laden, they all uniformly used that information to suggest that if the degradation of biodiversity continues at the current rate, the human race as a whole faces a catastrophe of epic proportions. One article, "Biodiversity and Ecosystem Functioning: Maintaining Natural Life Support Processes," which stresses the tentativeness of its conclusion and the vast amounts of research that need to be done to understand fully the relationship between ecosystem functioning and biodiversity, nevertheless concludes,

> Unprecedented changes are taking place in the ecosystems of the world, including species losses through local extinction, species additions through biological invasions, and wholesale changes in ecosystems that follow transformation of wildlands into managed ecosystems. These changes have a number of important effects on ecosystem processes. Recent evidence demonstrates that both the magnitude and stability of ecosystem functioning are likely to be significantly altered by declines in local diversity, especially when diversity reaches the low levels typical of managed ecosystems. Although a number of uncertainties remain, the importance of ecosystem services to human welfare requires that we adopt the prudent strategy of preserving biodiversity in order to safeguard ecosystem processes vital to society.

Clearly, in spite of multiple caveats raised throughout the article about the limits of scientific knowledge, the authors here issue a warning and suggest, in the name of prudence, that action be taken to safeguard the ecosystem. Such claims as these—which appeared in more or less dramatic terms throughout the readings—have the power to evoke a deep-seated fear in those students who took the claims of the scientists seriously. For in sum, these scientists seemed to claim that the human race faces, sometime within the twenty-first century, an environmental meltdown equivalent to nuclear winter.

But fear may not be the correct word. I think something more complicated, something more diffuse and pervasive like anxiety, may have been produced. I was not immune to this emotion myself. I became perturbed at the scientists' seemingly ambiguous claims: a) they seemed to know enough to make truly frightening claims, while b) also openly admitting that they didn't really know enough about biodiversity, that they didn't know even, for example, how many species there are. My own anxiety at these mixed messages became apparent one day when I concluded that the scientists writing these articles were, in fact, using fear as a way of obtaining increased funding for their own research. It is possible they wished to create an institute for the production of taxonomists.

This cynical and reductive reaction masked a form of anxiety pointed to by the psychoanalytic critic Slavoj Žižek:

> [I]t is impossible today to assume a moderate rational po-
> sition between scaremongering (ecologists who depict an
> impending universal catastrophe) and covering up (down-
> playing the dangers). The downplaying strategy can always
> emphasize the fact that scaremongering at best takes as
> certain conclusions which are not fully grounded in scien-
> tific observation; while the scaremongering strategy is fully
> justified in retorting that once it is possible to predict the
> catastrophe with full certainty, it will be, by definition, al-
> ready too late. The problem is there is no objective science
> or other way to acquire certainty about existence and ex-
> tent. . . . [T]here is in fact no way to establish the extent of
> the risk with certainty. (336)

Of course the scientists whose work I had students read were saying exactly this: given the limits of current knowledge there is no way "to establish the extent of the risk with certainty." This view was, in fact, part of what I hoped students might learn about the fourth order of consciousness and the scientific ethos that pervades it. Uncertainty and the capacity to live with it are built into the sci-entific ethos. I have heard scientists say this quite forcefully, and indeed, the articles I assigned demonstrated clearly scientists' aware-ness of the limits of their knowledge. This limitation is part of what I hoped students might learn by reading scientific topics.

But as my own cynical response to the readings indicates, this uncertainty, while on the one hand simply scientists' humble admis-sion of the limitations of their knowledge, was, on the other, aggra-vating and anxiety-producing, given the nature of the risk at hand: the potential for and possibility of complete ecological collapse. A scientist may live with uncertainty and have his or her self narcis-sistically affirmed in doing so, since unpredictability is a central element of the scientific enterprise. But for the ordinary nonscien-tist, who is not narcissistically invested in the role of scientist, the very element of uncertainty in the scientific accounts of biodiversity lends itself to two possible irrational responses.

Žižek's postmodern take on the problem indeed suggests there is no way for the autonomous self to find a moderate or rational position with respect to this particular issue. Rather, given the un-certainty, one must assume the position of either the "scaremonger" or the "downplayer." The scaremonger ignores the uncertainty in scientific reports to emphasize the need to do something now. The downplayer points to the uncertainty in scientific accounts as a way of suggesting the degree of the risk is far from clear. This division in outlook points also to something else: a possible rift in common sense. For surely the intensity of response to scientists' claims has to do with the implications of these claims for the activity of people in their daily lives. Should one change one's behavior relative to this possible crisis? Common sense, while it may function to hold to-gether the social order, cannot itself supply an answer to this ques-tion. Nor, for that matter, can science.

In formulating the assignment, I had been aware of this pos-sible problem. The uncertainty was one reason I decided that stu-dents should write summary. I had wanted them, in reading the articles, to become better acquainted with how scientists think and how their thinking involves the necessary element of uncertainty. I anticipated, from other classes that dealt with environmental issues, that if students engaged their subjective selves, the results would be just as Žižek predicts: arguments—or more precisely, opinions—that stated the world was about to end or that there was no problem whatsoever. And in-class discussion of the topic of biodiversity affirmed my anticipation: students fell roughly into exactly the camps described by Žižek.

A very few students simply ignored the assignment. They did not write summaries but instead gave their subjective or irrational responses. These responses, like the summaries I received, seemed largely unsatisfactory but for different reasons. While the summaries were frequently fragmented and disorganized, the more subjective responses were organized. But while the summaries did represent attempts to respond to the readings, the more subjective responses gave little indication that the articles had been read at all. Rather, the articles seemed a gross stimulus or the catalyst for the expression of an opinion the student had formed well before being assigned these readings. The readings hadn't, in other words, informed or deepened these responses one whit.

One student, for example, had clearly learned in the course of her previous education a good deal about the sad state of world ecology. She had taken this message to heart and believed it. But that was precisely the problem; her paper was simply an expression of belief. This student did believe the ecosystem was in deep danger; further she appeared to believe relatively little if anything could be done about the potential collapse. The ecosystem would break down, but she felt scientists would rescue the human race. They would build, in outer space, floating farms that would furnish nourishment and a home for species diversity. This strange image so startled me that I asked the student if she really believed such a thing would happen. She said yes, and that was why she was going to study science.

This student's paper and my brief talk with her made me sad. I seemed to be in the presence of a person who took ecological matters seriously and had concluded, on the basis of what she had been told, that the matter was very grave. She also seemed to feel that there was very little, if anything, an individual could do to impede the crisis, even though she recycled and tried to make ecologically conscious purchases. Eventually, perhaps within her lifetime, the earth would be, in effect, denatured. But hope still lay with them, the scientists, who would save us ultimately from ourselves, even though the situation in which we continued to live might appear, feel, and actually be scarcely human.

The Craft Approach and the Role of the "I"

The response from the student who expected the eventual loss of our planet's natural habitat, as well as the fractured and fragmented summaries from other students, made me wonder what in heaven's name I had been thinking when I put together the assignment. This is a rhetorical question; what I *had* been thinking I have already recorded. More to the point might be the following questions: What hadn't I been thinking? What had been going on at the more unconscious level? Wendy Bishop affords me a clue. She argues in "Writing Is/and Therapy," a chapter in *Teaching Lives,* that many instructors of writing may have embraced a craft approach to the teaching of writing "as a way to downplay the affective states students as writers negotiate when they begin to explore and express selves" (146).

Downplaying the affective states of students is precisely what I had been doing by asking students to write summary. But I hadn't quite sensed this downplaying meant pushing students toward a craft-oriented approach to writing. Bishop continues:

> Overall, I sense a profession-wide uneasiness regarding the connection of self to writing and from this uneasiness springs a substitution of attention: even our process workshops are under the sway of craft-based pedagogy and generally insist on the author-is-always-distinct-from-the-text ground rules from the first class onward. (145)

Implicit in the craft-oriented approach is a general insistence upon the author-is-always-distinct-from-the-text ground rule. At this point, I must balk and defend myself.

One can easily respond—quite reasonably and consciously—
that if teaching writing as craft implies a separation of self from text,
then so be it. Isn't that what academic writing—and the teaching
of it—is all about? For example, Charles Bazerman, in his seminal
article "What Written Knowledge Does," analyzes the discourse conventions or rhetorical moves in an article about science, Watson and
Crick's original note on DNA; one from the social sciences, Robert
K. Merton's "The Ambivalence of Scientists"; and one from the humanities, Geoffrey Hartman's "Blessing the Torrent: On Wordsworth's Later Style." In his conclusion, Bazerman writes,

> To recapitulate the major points of comparison among the
> three texts analyzed is to notice that the three statements
> of knowledge are three different things. In mediating real-
> ity, literature, audience, and self, each text seems to be
> making a different kind of move in a different kind of game.
> All three texts appear to show interest in phenomena which
> form the topics for the essays (as well as provide the titles).
> But the phenomena are not equally fixed prior to the es-
> says. (*Shaping* 46)

Bazerman seems to suggest that one's ability to make a knowledge
claim in a particular disciplinary area requires that one understand
the game one is playing. I go a step further to suggest that understanding the rules of the game one is playing is tantamount to understanding the way a knowledge claim must be crafted if it is to
be recognized as a knowledge claim. Moreover, Bazerman includes
self (along with reality, literature and audience) as one of the fac-
tors to be mediated in the game.

Of the kind of knowledge statement represented in Hartman's
analysis of Wordsworth's poem, Bazerman writes, "And Hartman's
game is open to even more idiosyncratic moves because the ground-
ing evidence is displaced from the game-board into the player; the
fundamental reality to be experience resides within the critic" (*Shaping* 48). Within the discipline of literary criticism at least, the self—
or the "fundamental reality . . . within the critic"—plays, relative

to the overall craft, a larger role than in science or social science writing. Following Bazerman's exposition, one can say that the self, as Bishop means it, simply does not appear in academic writing; even the self, as presented in literary criticism, is a form of rhetorical trope aimed at establishing a knowledge claim within a particular disciplinary context.

Bazerman's analysis of academic writing suggests that if one wishes to teach it, the thing to be most taught is the separation of self, as Bishop and I mean it, from the text. Indeed, I believe Bishop fudges on this point and places it, the most critical thing, in a parenthetical aside. She argues that writing teachers may be exposed to the less "curative" aspects of writing in part because they ask students to remove some defenses before "they have developed new equally necessary defenses (for instance, the agreement that what they say on paper is not synonymous with fact, feeling and life)" (146). Buried in that parenthetical "for instance" is, I believe, *the* agreement: that what one writes is not one's facts, feelings, life, or in other words, self.

These might be the quite rational and even conscious arguments of a person who is devoted to a craft-oriented approach to writing. But as I hope I have made clear by this point, I am not devoted to the craft approach; indeed my psychoanalytic approach presupposes some form of connection, whether conscious or unconscious, between the self of the writer and what he or she writes. And so, while I do not favor in a fundamental way the craft approach, the exigencies of my institutional situation—working with teaching assistants and attempting to respond to the design of Writing 2—moved me in a direction the implications of which I did not fully and consciously grasp. As I said, Bishop affords me a clue, a hint at what I had not been thinking. What I had unconsciously bought into was the fourth order of consciousness and its epistemological assumptions, especially as they were embodied in the design of Writing 2.

But because I hadn't consciously bought into the craft approach as the pedagogy most appropriate for teaching the fourth order of consciousness, I didn't, for example, severely penalize those students who wrote off the topic. And because I was able to put myself in the shoes of those students who wrote poor summaries, I was not inclined to add to their evident misery by penalizing them heavily either. Maybe for this reason, because I understood psychologically and accepted some responsibility for the quality of the students' writing, I did not experience with a single student those emotional scenes of anger, recrimination, or crying that Bishop reports in her article. In this light, I am inclined to argue that the craft approach, if fully and wholly embraced, may produce precisely that sort of emotionality it seeks to downplay by insisting that the author be distinct from the text.

Most people can understand the irritation that arises when they express something they believe is important to a person they take as important, only to have that person respond not to what they are saying but to the incorrect use of a word. This situation roughly is the relation of teacher to student as it is constructed, in the intersubjective field, with the craft approach. Students do become engaged willy-nilly in the act of writing as self-exploration, as Bishop suggests. And when they do, the particular quality of this self-exploration arises, especially for first-year students, from their institutional surround. Because teachers seek to distinguish text from the self, writing becomes self-exploration as an attempt by the student to find his or her particular relationship to this new environment.

Students self-explore because they are asked to experience the act of writing in a different way. In the course of this exploration, they may come across things about themselves that they previously did not know. When I teach something about politics, I am always surprised (and perhaps it is significant that I always am surprised) by the number of students who say they have never thought about their political view or position before. In thinking about it for the first time, and coming to know something about their relation to the world, they may realize that something significant has just happened to them..

The student in this light may experience the act of writing as a form of self-expression or, more exactly, as the expression of a self-realization. If that is the case, she or he most likely wishes to be understood. But understanding may be hard for the writing instructor if he or she assumes a craft approach. What the teacher sees is that the student's thesis is not clear or that the truth at which the student has arrived appears to be—and no doubt is—a truism so obvious as to scarcely be worth noting. The note in the margin indicating "cliché" next to the student's main point might be narcissistically wounding. And, if it is, this wounding may account, in part at least, for the emotionality that instructors who employ a craft orientation may experience.

The "I" as Ego Autonomy or Ego Dominance

Bishop's characterization of the craft approach as an attempt to downplay students' selves does not do justice to the in-depth psychological function of this approach. It is much better described purely and simply as a defense. For all the rational arguments that may be mustered in its favor, it acts primarily as a defense against having the instructor's narcissistic investment in the fourth-order epistemology (and through that, his or her narcissistic investment in the university itself) brought into question. Since, in light of one's narcissistic investment in the fourth order of consciousness, one is acting reasonably, rationally, and rightly in teaching writing as craft, one is ill-positioned to experience students' emotionality (i.e., expressions of their selves) as anything but irrational.

The problem, of course, is not instructors' narcissistic investment in the fourth order of consciousness. If they had not invested in it and come to experience it, they would not know what it was. The problem is, developmentally and psychologically, that in buying into the fourth order, instructors also buy into the prevailing pedagogy. This pedagogy, which Henry Giroux describes as positivistic, seeks to teach, in a hidden and not so hidden curriculum, the distinctions between fact and value, object and subject.

These are epistemological distinctions, but implicit in them is a psychology relative to knowledge and its acquisition. Roughly put, this psychology suggests that if objectivity, or the truth, is to be found, values must be eliminated from the scene (of the observer) and the subject must somehow void its subjectivity if it is accurately to represent the object. In short, this psychology establishes between subject and object a purely epistemological relationship. The relationship between knower and known is not an intersubjective relationship. If one is to be objective, there can be no question, as with something like hypnosis, that the answer one gets from the object was placed there by the subject.

Recognition of the object as object (i.e., as distinct from the "self") means not an elimination of subjectivity but rather the establishment of a particular self or psychological relationship to the other. Some better sense of what I mean may be afforded by a distinction Kohut makes between ego dominance and ego autonomy:

> There is a place for ego autonomy: the rider *off* the horse; man as he reflects coolly and dispassionately, particularly as he scrutinizes the data of his observations. But there is a place also for ego-dominance; the rider *on* the horse; man as he responds to the forces within himself, as he shapes his goals and forms his major reactions to his environment; man as an effective participant on the state of history. In the narcissistic realm, in particular, ego dominance increases our ability to react with the full spectrum of emotions, with disappointment and rage and with feelings of triumph, controlledly, but not necessarily restrainedly. (*Self Psychology* 129)

The implicit psychology of the positivistic pedagogy, I believe, is that of ego autonomy, the rider off the horse of the passions and away from the sway of narcissism. If this psychology is implicit in the positivistic pedagogy of the university, then it is easy to see why instructors of writing are unable to recognize the subjectivities of their students.

If an instructor has narcissistically invested in the fourth order of consciousness, in that particular and peculiar way of thinking, and if she has embraced the psychology implicit in the positivistic pedagogy, then the instructor simply does not experience her self as a subjectivity. Rather, she is an objective knower—or is at least striving for that position—and what she has to offer the student is the truth, whatever that might be, relative to the knowledge she has. To the extent that the instructor has narcissistically invested in this conception of her task, she inevitably begins to project on others the view of the psyche, as self off the horse of the passions, implicit in the positivistic pedagogy.

The instructor's students simply don't seem to get it, and she can't figure out why. She can't figure out why because she has projected on students that view of the ego that she, at the fourth order of consciousness, has already acquired. This is the bottom-line mistake: the projection of a particular conception of the self into students, when that self is precisely what needs to be developed. No wonder the instructor is flustered and frustrated. If she, largely unconsciously, assumes that students have egos capable of dispassionately surveying their surroundings, then their failure to understand must be the result of some perversity or irrationality. Their very emotionality, as an expression of their subjectivities, is then experienced as resistance to her teachings. And if she experiences students' emotionality as a resistance to her teaching, she is ill-positioned to extend to the student any empathy or to begin to acknowledge that her pedagogy may contribute to the resistance she experiences.

This does not mean at all that instructors of writing should abandon the attempt to teach students the fact-value, self-other, subject-object distinctions. The question, rather, is how to do it. Frankly, I do not believe there is such a thing as the autonomous ego or the rider off the horse of the passions, as a final or absolute state or, for that matter, as a state that any human being has ever achieved. Instead, this state or condition of facing the truth as truth, no matter what it says or wherever it might lead, represents very much an ideal. It is, indeed, a heroic ideal, one worth pursuing. But turning over rocks or sticking one's nose into strange places just so that one may know (and for no other reason) what is there is not every person's cup of tea.

The question then is how to teach this particular ideal that is embedded in the structures of the university as modernist institution. One way clearly not to teach it is for the instructor to act as if he is it. If, in other words, his self-relation to the role of teacher is informed by a narcissistic investment in the idea of the self off the horse of the passions, he is not likely to present this position, in his embodiment, as an ideal. If he embodies the rider off the horse of the passions as an ideal, he must do so not from the position of ego autonomy but from the position of ego dominance. As such, he presents knowledge not as that which has been achieved but as an ongoing form of activity. For, according to Kohut, the rider on the horse represents "man as he responds to the forces within himself, as he shapes his goals and forms his major reactions to his environment; man as an effective participant on the stage of history" (*Self Psychology* 129).

Turning over a rock just to see what is there could pose a risk to one's hands. For some persons, it may seem even an instance of irrationality. Or as the commonplace has it, better to let sleeping dogs lie. But better to risk the charge of irrationality than to present the ideal of knowing as if it were not an expression of subjectivity. If one takes this approach, it might be possible to present the ideal of ego autonomy as something possibly meaningful, as something that might guide and give purpose to one's actions, as something possibly even noble and heroic, requiring for its realization its own particular kind of courage and fortitude. If this tack is taken, some students may themselves take it up in varying degrees of intensity and commitment as an ideal that might vitalize them as sustaining selfobject.

Extrospection: The Subject-Object Distinction as a Psychological Relation

The psychoanalyst D. W. Winnicott states flatly that no individual is in direct "contact" with reality (*Human Nature* 114–15). I believe that statement is true, though to be clear, it has not always been my belief, and even now, I am still trying to figure out exactly what it might mean. But this idea—that no one is in direct contact with reality—is one reason I continue to value the ideal of ego autonomy. Through learning the fact-value, self-object distinctions implicit in the ideal of ego autonomy, one may also come to realize that what one sees is frequently shaped by one's beliefs, one's views, and one's experience at both conscious and unconscious levels. One might then come to see, at least provisionally in moments of doubt and skepticism, that what one experiences as real might be largely unconscious and narcissistically maintained projections.

The difficulty here, developmentally and pedagogically, is that the subject-object, fact-value distinctions implicit in the notion of ego autonomy are taught from the perspective of the positivistic pedagogy as a priori concepts to be inculcated downward, as it were, into the intellect of students. What this pedagogy simply cannot see is that the capacity to be objective requires that the individual assert a certain psychological or subjective relation to the world (not an epistemological relation, whatever that might be). Kohut gives a name to this particular relation; he calls it "extrospection."

Extrospection is an odd word, various forms of which I have seen in various places in psychoanalytic literature. Kohut does not stop to define what he might mean by it. But paired with its twin, introspection, extrospection is a kind of psychological relation. The former is a relation of the self to its inward states as it attempts to gather knowledge about those states, and the latter is a psychological relation to the external world, posited by the relation itself as possibly external. Clearly, as a psychological relationship, extrospection does not imply that the individual is in direct contact with the real, only that his or her psychological relationship to what he or she takes to be real has changed. In ordinary lived experience, in the intersubjective world of common sense, one experiences reality as that which affords the basis for action; in the extrospective relation, one experiences the world as a possible source of knowledge.

The cultivation of the capacity for extrospection appears critical to self-authorship as a conception of the self somehow distinct from its relationships, as something that, in its own activity, generates meaning. From the perspective of the cultivation of this capacity, "I don't understand" must precede "I understand." The difficulty here, however, is that at the level of third order of consciousness, everything in the shared reality of common sense is already understood. Academic subject matter, theories, and disciplinarity, however, shake up the shared understanding of common sense.

When a student says, "I don't understand what Kant says," one may assume that at some level, he does understand. He has understood at least enough to feel, however unconsciously, that his previous shared and assumed understanding at the third order of consciousness has been disrupted. Frequently the student is unable to say what precisely in Kant he doesn't understand. He is confused and unable to locate the source of his confusion. This situation suggests that he is confused not by Kant but by something *in* Kant that has altered, however minimally, his third-order understanding of the world of common sense.

At this point—when the student does not understand and is unable to indicate the source of the confusion—we may say that the student has narcissistically merged with Kant. One basic though nondevelopmental way to break this merger is to conclude (*a*) that Kant is stupid or (*b*) that the student is stupid. What the student must do—by no means easy—is, on the basis of the narcissistic merger, to move in two directions at once. She must introspect in an attempt to locate the belief or idea that Kant disrupts, but to find this disrupted belief, she must also extrospect Kant. She must maintain the bare possibility at least that Kant may be saying something different from what she experiences him as saying. Only if she is able to maintain the bare possibility that the source of her confusion does not emanate from Kant will she be positioned to acknowledge that the confusion, in fact, lies in her own beliefs, notions, ideals, and thoughts.

Grasping the Concept: Potentials for Narcissistic Destabilization

This process, already complicated, becomes even more so if the student's capacity to extrospect—and to express that extrospection in language—requires that he reformulate his relation to language. What I mean may be suggested by returning to students' struggles with the topic of biodiversity. In pointing previously to the fragmentation in students' summaries, I failed to indicate that some students wrote decent summaries. In those papers I detected signs of self-authorship. All of the summaries were constructed around three obvious points clearly announced in the readings for the unit: what biodiversity is, its benefits (to humanity), and what is happening to it today. Every paper I received included a section on its benefits. Here is a passage about the benefits from a student paper that demonstrates self-authorship:

> On the most primal level, biodiversity provides humans with the basic tenets of survival: food, shelter and clothing. In terms of food, biodiversity forms the backbone and infrastructure of our entire food chain. All commercial food products, ranging from corn to alcohol, originate from some type of living organism. Thus it follows that severe disruptions to the natural world would have major consequences to our everyday diet. In addition, it is important to realize that the rest of the animal kingdom also has a delicate food chain, and even the slightest disturbances can cause great effects. For example, in the Gulf of Alaska, a small change in weather resulted in severe domino effect that permeated the entire ocean habitat, resulting in the near extinction of once abundant sea otters. Besides food, biodiversity provides the clothes on our back. Popular materials like cotton, flax, and rattan all are derived from various species of plants. Also, different plants, like trees, palm fronds, or bamboo poles are all sources of shelter for a great deal of people and animals.

Here is another passage more or less on the same point from a student paper that does not demonstrate self-authorship:

> Biodiversity is essential to all living creatures, including humans. We rely on the natural world for almost all of our needs. For example, corn is the third most important grain to human societies. Without studying the different naturally occurring varieties of corn, humans would not have been able to produce a perennial crop that is also disease

resistant. Without this variety found in nature, humans would not posses the ability to grow enough corn to supply the necessary amount. Aspirin, which has been used by millions of people over centuries, is based on the molecular structure of part of the willow tree. It is now made in a factory, but this shows how much can be gained by biodiversity. The first antibiotic, Penicillium, was derived from a mold that was originally used to flavor cheese. These are some of the most important medicines in human history, all derived from nature. Different species of plants and animals have millions of years to evolve and produce chemicals, which can be used against viruses, bacteria and many other human problems. Many species that could be beneficial to human societies may have already been lost due to human actions. These species and their benefits will never be known.

One might say of the first example that it demonstrates a hint of voice. The second doesn't. The first example is relatively well organized about a single heading and uses transitional phrases to establish its secondary or subsidiary points. The information is given a hierarchy. In the second example, no hierarchy is apparent.

From my psychoanalytic point of view, these rhetorical features mark a difference between self-authorship and a relative failure to assume it. Why is the first writer able to assume the position of self-authorship and the second not? I don't have the faintest idea, and I doubt that without extensive psychological investigation, I would be able to determine how and why the first writer can, perhaps prematurely, assume the position of self-authorship.

But, as I suggested, the movement to self-authorship may involve not a shift in epistemology precisely but, in addition and perhaps more significant, a shift in the individual's psychological relationship to language. Admittedly my thoughts here are speculative. But when I look at my students' responses to the topic of biodiversity, it seems that the movement to self-authorship requires that students come to view words as concepts. Or to follow Anne Bertoff, students must come to understand that language always "abstracts." Language is inherently conceptual. Beginning students, however, understand language as names for things and, by the same token, assume names are things. In students' writings on biodiversity, I found sentences of the following kind:

- Because of biodiversity there are many benefits that scientists have found to be useful to mankind.
- Biodiversity relates every living organism and exposes the fragility of the earth's ecosystems.
- Biodiversity is the variety of all life forms and the complex interaction of the elements of this variety with each other in the ecosystem.

In the first example, biodiversity appears not only as a thing but also as an active thing. Biodiversity appears to impel scientists to find in it many useful things. In the second, again, biodiversity appears an active agent in its own right. Biodiversity "relates." The last appears closer to a standard definition. But, in fact, biodiversity is not the variety of all life forms. Words are not things, and things are not words.

Biodiversity is not a thing but a concept. Relative to the language of science, it is an operational concept; it carves out, in the disciplinary terrain, a space for study or exploration. Biodiversity as a concept is intended to shift one's vision in a certain direction. It does not carve out some new area in the real. The variety of plant and animal species the significance of which it seeks to indicate was already there long before the word. Instead, biodiversity seeks to carve out a space for particular study, as a form of directed activity, within the already constituted disciplinary realm of environmental and ecological studies. The word is not a thing. Rather the force of the word lies in its conceptual power, a power it exercises not relative to things but to the reconceiving of the discipline of environmental or ecological studies.

It is significant that the student whose work does demonstrate a degree of self-authorship began his paper with the line "Biodiversity is the current buzzword being tossed around the scientific realm these days." This line says a great deal about the student's relation to the topic and to language. Biodiversity, he knows, is a word, not a thing. Moreover, the word, somewhat disparagingly called a buzzword, has no agency. It does not shape or impel; rather, people in the scientific realm "toss" it around. This student knows something about concepts. He knows they are used by human beings; they have no agency of their own. In effect, he knows what his capacity for self-authorship implies, that concepts make meanings. And because he knows this, the student is able to engage the topic "extrospectively," as a disciplinary realm of knowledge and as something other than himself.

Viewed developmentally and psychoanalytically, language functions as a selfobject not just for students but for everyone who occupies the third order of consciousness (and we all do). One narcissistically merges with the word. It is not outside oneself or inside, for that matter; it is part of the intersubjective world of common sense. When I am driving on the freeway and a friend says, "Watch out for that cop over there," the word *cop* does my thinking for me. I don't have to ask my friend why he says "watch out," and even though I may not see the cop over there, I don't need the significance of "over there" explained.

As I said, the word *cop* does my thinking for me. I do not mean this metaphorically. Rather, psychologically, the word has agency; it initiates a possible pattern of behavior. I may, at a minimum, glance at my speedometer to see whether I am going too fast. I may then slow down or change lanes to increase my distance from the cop. The word *cop* here is clearly not a concept pointing me in a particular disciplinary direction. It is a selfobject, which, depending on my circumstances, may be momentarily destabilizing and even produce the experience of an affect, as in, "Boy, do I hate cops."

This example represents the usual and daily relationship of the individual psyche to words. Words have agency and do our thinking for us. The movement, however, into the fourth order of consciousness requires that one assume an entirely different relationship to language. One might imagine, for example, students being asked, in a class on government and order, "Are cops necessary?"

Here the student must look at cops as a concept and argue whether they are essential relative to the maintenance of order. This line of investigation, further, may lead the student into a consideration of the purposes of government, and that in turn to a consideration of whether government is necessary. But to begin this move at all, the student must be able to call into question his or her selfobject relation to the word *cop*.

I believe a double destabilization may occur here. First, the student must doubt or, more likely, repress his selfobject relation to cops. Second, if the student does repress his selfobject relations in which may be latent strong affective charges, he is left facing the concept of the cop as something incomprehensible or indifferent to his psychological reality and, in that respect, as narcissistically wounding. I think here of my former student Peter, whom I interviewed at some length about his particular writing block. Peter felt great anxiety when he wrote because he said he felt as if he were facing a monolith.

He had in mind a particular monolith, the one that appears at the beginning of the film *2001: A Space Odyssey*. The monolithic quality of the writing experience appeared to be, in Peter's case, somehow related to his problem with page length. He had great difficulty understanding why one paper should be of this length and another of that. He experienced page length as arbitrary but seemed also to assume that there was some intelligence, some larger shaping force behind it. (For more on Peter's particular writing block, see Tingle, "Peter and the Monolith.") Peter, when he wrote, seemed to experience not as a continuum but as a disjuncture his relation to word as thing and thing as word. At the same time, since he appeared unable to find any self-relation to the topic at hand, he was faced with the concept as monolith.

Through this analysis, I am able to make somewhat better psychological sense of the mysterious line "Because of biodiversity there are many benefits that scientists have found to be useful to mankind." First, as I have indicated, the student, occupying the third order of consciousness, imparts agency to the concept. The student attempts to let the word do his thinking for him, in the same way that he might with the warning to watch out for the cop. The difficulty here, however, is that the word *biodiversity* is a concept just as the word *cop* in "are cops necessary" is a concept. The word used in this way cannot do the student's thinking for him. After the phrase "because of biodiversity," the student is left completely stranded. In effect, he faces the monolith and is disoriented. "There are" springs to the rescue as an attempt to assert some connection to the bare concept. But as connections go, it is very, very weak. Does the "there are" point back to "Because of biodiversity" or point forward to "many benefits." In effect this weak connection allows the student to turn his back on, or repress, the bare concept while still allowing it, unconsciously, to do his thinking for him. The difficulty here is that the concept, if it functions unconsciously as a selfobject, ceases to be concept at all for the individual.

Learning Theory and Knowing Less: Potentials for Destabilization

I recollect from my own time in college an experience that can shed light on the developmental passage I am describing here. I remember having anticipated with some excitement a series of three lectures to be given on the Russian Revolution. My interest perhaps arose from my long infatuation with Russian novels. When the lectures concluded, I was, however, disappointed in a palpable way. The lectures, as far as I could tell, had added up to nothing. Though I could not have said it or even thought it then, each of the lectures had been delivered from a different theoretical or disciplinary perspective. One had been more historical and had dealt with the bread riots. A second had been more sociological and dealt with the role of serfs and serfdom in the events leading up to the revolution. The third, more political, concerned the various parties and their conflicts at the moment of the revolution.

My sense of disappointment I believe arose from my relative rootedness in the third order of consciousness. I experienced words as things. I had unconsciously assumed that the lectures on the Russian Revolution would evoke an event. Instead I left the lectures with an unsettling sense that there had been no such event called the Russian Revolution. I still believed that something like it had happened, but what exactly and whether it could still be called the Russian Revolution, I was not sure. Take, for example, the simple matter of dates. From the lectures, given the different perspectives, it was hard to determine when exactly the revolution had started, and if this was the case, how could one call it an event, for surely an event had a distinguishable beginning, middle, and end.

In *The Psychology of the Imagination,* Sartre argues that we are able to take a tour of a real object. I see this tree as a real tree and am aware that I am situated relative to it so that I can see only one side of the tree; to see the real thing, I must tour it and walk around the tree. As I walk around the tree, I see it as a series of profiles. Moreover, relative to the real thing, as we tour it, Sartre says, we may experience surprise. We may be surprised for example that one side of the tree has been struck by lightning or another side covered with moss. The real object Sartre contrasts with the imaginary object, a "tree," say, constructed in imagination. One cannot, he says, be surprised by an imaginary object; further, he argues one can learn nothing from an image, because our knowledge of it is there all at once and put there by our imagination (8–14).

I had attended the series of lectures thinking I would be given a tour of the Russian Revolution as a real object. Instead, I found out that the Russian Revolution is an imaginary object. Or more precisely, I found out that the Russian Revolution was several imaginary objects or theories. I learned exactly nothing about the Russian Revolution from these theories, understood as imaginary objects. The knowledge the images afford had been put there in the theory all at once. In a dim way, I began to sense that the assumptions one makes about the objects of one's study constitute the subject as an imaginary object. If one could grasp those assumptions, the object itself would become transparently known.

But while I learned nothing about the Russian Revolution from the theories that constructed it as imaginary object, this experience of not learning anything was part of learning the more critical thing. I was gradually gaining the capacity to move out of the third order of consciousness into the fourth, however momentarily or occasionally. About this time, I realized that if I was to endure this experience of learning nothing about real objects—and I remember having said this out loud to a friend—I would have to develop "ambiguity tolerance."

Psychoanalytically, I would now say that the experience of the lectures on the Russian Revolution and numerous other experiences like it destabilized my narcissistically informed relation to the third order of consciousness. At this level, I had assumed that *Russian Revolution* was a term for a real thing. I learned, however, not from the individual lectures (which taught me nothing) but from the experience as a whole that the Russian Revolution—what it was or what it had been—was ambiguous. Moreover, as the word *tolerance* implies, coming to understand this was not simply an intellectual matter. It involved me at an affective level. I did not like, in an elemental way, what I was experiencing. Learning to tolerate ambiguity was almost like learning to tolerate a poison. Over time, through acceptance of ambiguity in little doses, I assumed I would reach a point at which it no longer affected me.

This tolerance was, I believe, developmentally the main thing to be learned. *Ambiguity* and *uncertainty* may serve as epistemological terms for the psychological capacity to extrospect. Ambiguity and uncertainty became for me the bare other. In addition, by developing this extrospective capacity, I came better to understand the function of theory as means by which I might assert a relationship of knowledge to this bare other. I was, at this point, positioned to move, however occasionally and momentarily, into self-authorship. Since there was nothing known, then I might construct knowledge. I could invent meanings, as long, that is, as I was able to shape my assumptions in a way that might be perceived and understood by my professors.

Kohut, Hamlet, and the Rigors of Development

In the foregoing, I have used psychoanalysis to provide a better sense of what I think is going on for students, at conscious and unconscious levels, as they attempt the developmental move enjoined by the university. Admittedly this has meant looking at some pretty murky stuff. I am involved in at least some degree of murk when I hypothesize that my pedagogical approach may construct the intersubjective terrain of the classroom in ways that end up being mostly narcissistically informed reflections of me.

But there is murk and then there is murk. If one inhabits the fourth order of consciousness, as I sometimes provisionally do, one simply wants epistemologically *to know* what is out there and what is in here. From this perspective, the psychoanalytic intersubjective terrain may appear painfully, even frightfully murky. But as postmodernism (and psychoanalysis) remind us, the self-authoring position of the autonomous ego is itself an illusion and, as such, tends to generate its own forms of murk. I turned for help to psychoanalysis because no matter how hard I employed my reason, I simply couldn't understand some of the things I saw in my writing classes.

Psychoanalysis produced not murk but clarity. For whatever personal reason, I have always been drawn to a nondirected mode of teaching. Perhaps because of that attraction, I remember having received, at a time when I was just beginning to formulate my subjective approach, a number of students' papers that suggested and sometimes directly stated that the hero of *Hamlet* is Horatio. No doubt I had asked for this by telling my students that they could respond subjectively. But whether I asked for it or not, I had to wonder how a student could conclude that Horatio was the hero.

Maybe this was simply a sort of default position. Horatio was by default the hero because students felt that Hamlet wasn't. Hamlet was crazy and, as such, not hero material. I didn't experience Hamlet, however, as crazy. What were my students responding to that I wasn't? I received some illumination when sometime later I ran across the following passage in Kohut:

> Hamlet's death is the triumphant fulfillment of his reconstituted nuclear self, and his weaknesses, hesitations and temporary failures are like the climber's toils and sighs to reach the peak. Horatio's touching last words ("goodnight,

sweet prince") are not the adequate response to great achievement. They are a concession to the sentimental needs of that part of the audience that cannot tolerate the identification with the triumph of undiluted heroic self-fulfillment. (*Self Psychology* 43)

These remarks afford me a clue. Perhaps students rejected Hamlet as hero, not precisely because they experienced Hamlet as crazy but because projecting him as crazy served as a defense against a full identification "with the triumph of undiluted heroic self-fulfillment."

Why might some persons not be able so to identify? Because, Kohut writes, "[o]ur selves have become too fragile." Leaving aside the more metapsychological implications of Kohut's assertion for our understanding of the modern psyche, his claim seemed to me to clarify. The ability or inability to identify with Hamlet's fate had something to do with students' selves. Whether students were able to write convincingly about the hero of *Hamlet* had less to do, then, with students' intellects or with their smarts and much more to do with their selves and their emotional being. As a teacher of *Hamlet,* I drew from this a single inference. I could present any manner of rational arguments why Hamlet should be regarded as a hero, but these very arguments would only further destabilize students who were unprepared fully to identify with Hamlet. And to find stability, they would locate in the play Horatio as hero.

Hamlet is hard to identify with in part because his story is the story of a self that goes to hell in a handbasket. He was an "idealist," Kohut claims, who learns something that is destructive of his idealizing relationship to his situation. Consequently, his self is threatened at its root. He can deny everything, of course. But he doesn't. Instead, as Kohut argues, a great deal of the play—the middle part, the temporizing part—presents a picture of the agony Hamlet's self undergoes as it attempts to reconstitute itself. Kohut writes,

The enormous task of rebuilding a new self that is structured in conformity with the changed world in which he finds himself absorbs all his energies during most of the

action of the play. It strains his psychic powers to the ut-
most, leading to a state of diffuse tensions of which his
(pseudo-) insanity, his outbursts of rage, his sarcasm, and
his seeming confusion are either direct manifestations or
indirect symptoms. The inner task, however, is eventually
accomplished, and his new disillusioned self is built. (43)

Once this work is done, Hamlet is ready. His death is not, as Kohut
says, a punishment but a fulfillment. Hamlet's life ends at its fullest
point. That's the tragedy and the triumph. What would *Hamlet* be
had Hamlet lived?

Hamlet's story is a story of self-development. He faces the enormous task of rebuilding a new self that is structured in conformity
with the changed world in which he finds himself. If I am correct,
this is the task too that faces students upon entry to the university.
They must in effect rebuild themselves "in conformity with the
changed world in which they find [themselves]." Most students,
thankfully, will not come into the kind of direct and immediate
contact with evil that Hamlet does, nor is the transition to the university as shockingly abrupt as the one Hamlet experiences. But if
students are to adjust to the world in which they find themselves,
they will, at relatively surface levels of the self, need to call into
question and loosen their narcissistically informed allegiances to
certain ideals, values, beliefs, and conceptions. This questioning, in
turn, for those who take up the task, will require a rebuilding of self.
And if students are able to rebuild their selves, they might experience their education as a narcissistically sustaining triumph.

3 / Theory, Selfobjects, and Falseness

The Rage to Teach

I would like to outline the primary "take-home" lesson of what follows *for* the writing instructor. The writing class as transitional environment is not simply a place where the student might develop and be restored. It is also where the writing instructor might develop and experience self-restoration. Indeed, creating this environment for students seems inextricably bound up with the instructor's efforts to restore his or her self. But what would the restoration of the self of the writing instructor precisely mean? And why, even, would such restoration be necessary?

To begin to answer these questions, I must back up a bit. Teachers—true teachers, those who care about what they are doing, those who actually see themselves as in some way changing students' minds—are drawn to the activity for psychological reasons. These motivations of course may, at the deepest level, vary considerably from person to person, but at a more surface level, true teachers teach because they believe they know something valuable that students too should know. Consequently, the true teacher, in the words of the psychoanalyst M. Robert Gardner, is frequently possessed of a "furor to teach." Gardner writes,

> Without the furor to teach, true teachers are most unlikely to move themselves or their students. But the line between helpful furor and harmful is full of lost edges, and, consequently, of lost teachers and students. Beset by so many furors to teach and finding so many students ignorant of

what they feel compelled to teach, true teachers, despite
their grand respect for the human mind—if not for many
particular minds—often find their students' minds to be
vacuums. . . . Moreover, when students rebuff their efforts
to impart the necessary wisdom, rebuffed true teachers are
moved to higher and higher levels of furor; furor begets
opposition begets furor begets opposition and so on. (6)

It would be a mistake to think Gardner is simply making fun of the
true teacher and his furor. Certainly, he is joshing, but he is also
pointing to something more serious.

In that word *furor* and in his description of the furor begetting
opposition begetting furor, I think Gardner is pointing to the possibility, perhaps inherent in the act of teaching, of what Kohut calls
narcissistic rage. Narcissistic rage may arise from experiences rang-
ing from "such trivial occurrences as fleeting annoyance when someone fails to reciprocate our greetings or does not respond to our joke
to such ominous derangements as the furor of the catatonic and the
grudges of paranoiac" (*Self Psychology* 142). Depending on the stability of the individual self, even very trivial slights or insults may
give rise to an upsurge of narcissistic rage. And this rage, Kohut
continues, has a particular "psychological flavor":

> The need for revenge, for righting a wrong, for undoing a
> hurt by whatever means, and a deeply anchored, unrelent-
> ing compulsion in the pursuit of all these aims, which gives
> no rest to those who have suffered narcissistic injury—
> these are the characteristic features of narcissistic rage in
> all its forms and which set it apart from other kinds of ag-
> gression. (143)

Not all teachers are motivated at the unconscious level by narcissistic rage or some desire to right a wrong long ago experienced
and impossible to undo. I only point to the potentials in the act of
teaching for narcissistic injury and how that might feed into what
Gardner calls furor and I call rage. If, in other words, one believes

one knows something of value that students should know, one is certainly positioned to experience possible narcissistic wounding. One wishes one's students, in their performance as students, to mirror or narcissistically affirm the value that one attempts to assert. But they don't always. In fact, frequently they don't.

Teachers might not want to admit it, but students have the power to hurt or destabilize the teacher. Students don't, of course, necessarily mean to do this, or let's say, in most cases, hurting the teacher is not perhaps uppermost in students' minds. But when one works hard and does one's very best to show students how, for example, to write an organized paper, and the papers one finally receives are mostly not organized, one may feel hurt. Or in class when it seems I have to repeat myself four times to be heard once, I might feel hurt. Indeed, if I were a child and my parents treated me in this way, I might conclude that they don't really care about me.

One could of course say that having students who don't pay attention or don't seem to get what one delivers simply comes with the territory of being a teacher. But what does it mean? Doesn't it mean that one simply accepts as a reality that students don't listen and mostly they don't understand what one says? And if this is the case, what precisely could be the purpose of persisting as a teacher? No, if being a teacher means not being able to teach or being ignored when one tries to do so, it represents not a reality but simply a very effective rationalization of being hurt. The rationalization stabilizes the self in its relation to its role as teacher and the narcissistic wounding that seems to come from the exercise of this role.

The true teacher, as Gardner puts it, doesn't stop trying to teach even if he or she feels that it is mostly impossible, because he or she is possessed by a furor. And this furor, or rage, that results from having been hurt can, as Kohut suggests, be very, very motivating. Rage, the desire for revenge, the wish to right a wrong, can lead, Kohut argues, to an unrelenting compulsion in pursuit of one's aims. I have felt such rage and still do. I have had occasion in hallway conversations with my colleagues to refer to students in terms most unflattering to them. I have, on occasion, felt very hurt by my students' seeming inability to value what I value or to understand what

I ask of them. And rather than admit my own narcissistic vulner-ability—that I have indeed been hurt by them—I break my inter-subjective relation to the students and rationalize my rage.

Rage, in this context, may serve as the last refuge of purpose. The desire for revenge may keep one at it for a very long time, as rage begets oppositions begets rage. One is able to find a meaning in what one does, but as Kohut suggests, the desire for revenge may be compulsive, even addictive. One tinkers with one's writing as-signments. One writes it this way and then rewrites it that way. One is endlessly restless about one's assignments. One keeps thinking that if only one could hit the perfect formulation, the most exact phrasing, students would know, as if transfixed by a brilliant light, what is being asked. But when the results come in, one is left with the feeling of having spit into the wind, having poured good money after bad, and having wasted one's time kicking a dead horse.

While rage may serve as the last refuge of purpose, it also de-feats the purpose. In other words, while unconscious rage and its more conscious rationalizations may stabilize the self of the teacher, that self clearly has experienced destabilization and fragmentation. The teacher's self, in this instance, requires restoration or restabili-zation by some affective means other than rage. Rage can, as I have suggested, provide temporary solace. But if furor begets opposition, rage may tend to produce only further narcissistic wounding.

That is only one problem. Another is that rage tends to limit one's flexibility. One is tied compulsively to certain practices. In my attempts to explain myself to students, I have mistaken turning up the volume for increased clarity. Or, let's say, increased clarity (here exactly is what I want!) may amount psychologically to turning up the volume. But there is something paradoxical in the idea that stu-dents may hear what one has to say if one manages to deafen them.

Gardner, in his own form of paradox, suggests a possible av-enue toward self-restoration: "[W]hen trying to teach, try not to." If one is a true teacher, this statement might seem simply a formula for giving up entirely. But note, Gardner does not say, "Stop teach-ing." Because, for him, trying not to teach itself has an educative purpose: "[T]ry not to teach till, after trying not to, you can fathom a piece of the drift of the hidden questions of the person you hope to teach whatever you hope to teach." Or to put the matter in terms I find more familiar, try not to teach till you understand or emphatically see those things that might be operating for the student at a hidden level, sometimes deeply buried, sometimes just outside the reach of consciousness. This is pretty much my formula for the writing class as transitional environment.

Such an approach to teaching may prove restorative for the student and for the teacher. Nothing can quell the fire of the rage to teach—and nothing should—and nothing can soothe the sting of narcissistic wounding when one's aims and goals do not appear to have been realized. But one's goals may be placed on another footing if one conceives of them not so much as the attempt to teach what must be known but as the creation of an environment that might make more possible a move in students' self-development. The instructor—or more precisely, the very self of the instructor— is at the center of this environment.

And as this center, part of one's aim is to evaluate one's aims. One listens in part to see whether one's aims have produced enough space for hearing and understanding. If not—or if one keeps hearing over and over again the same thing—one may change one's aims, if only slightly. This change, however, requires that one listen not simply to one's students but also to oneself. And in this way, the self of the writing instructor might be restored.

I have employed psychoanalysis as a way of somehow getting past my own rage to teach. It's important that I do; otherwise what students may be experiencing as they attempt to learn what I teach may remain out of earshot. And if student's self-experiences remain out of earshot, I am ill-positioned to recognize my own self-experiences as teacher. This statement may seem paradoxical, but it is not. Most instructors do not recognize the rage in their rage to teach. The rage, still there and unconsciously buried, does not rise to the instructor's consciousness, because the very way he or she conceives of the pedagogical relationship shields the instructor against any conscious awareness of possible wounding by students.

But teachers are wounded every day, and hearing this wounding is not at all hard if one listens. One hears, "I had a crappy class today." One also hears, sometimes explicitly, "because they are a pack of idiots." Or "because they lack civility." Or "because they have not been raised properly." Or "because the entire educational system is in shambles." Or "because they have been brainwashed by the media." Or "because they seem to lack any attention span." It's hard for teachers to honestly express their feelings about students. One reason for this lack of honesty might be that if instructors did voice their feelings, one might hear a good deal of rage. And just below this rage, barely audible but still there, is, "They hurt me!"

This admission of pain might prove, however, an embarrassment to all, perhaps even a sign that one is unfit to be a teacher. For some reason, teachers are not supposed to be hurt, but if they are, they are to keep a stiff upper lip, suck it up, and do so with the absolute conviction that even if it hurts, they are nonetheless doing the right thing. In this instance, the instructor's theory, or idea, or simple conventional acceptance of what has been done serves as a stabilizing selfobject. And the more one believes or invests one's narcissistic energy in the rightness of what one does, the less one is inclined to feel hurt. Those hurt, though one does not hear it, are students who are as they are, perhaps because they are "postliterate."

The theories of what one does or should do as a writing teacher can be sophisticated and powerful. They may emanate from the highest levels of the authority structure of one's discipline; or they may be backed up with impressive empirical data or embody the latest intellectual trend. Or they may be implicit in the very institutional structures of the writing program in which one works. In the last instance particularly, it behooves one to pay attention to the theory, especially if one wants to do what one is supposed to do. These theories are important because even if they do represent simply ad hoc rationalizations of institutional realities embraced more for PR purposes than for anything else, they help the teacher to know what he or she needs to do to fit in. And they may act psychologically for instructors as stabilizing selfobjects, which also defensively protect teachers from narcissistic wounding at the hands of their students.

A defense mechanism is implicit in two such theories. Taken together, the two theories represent, for me, the Scylla and Charybdis through which the instructor who wishes to construct the writing class as transitional environment must steer. They seem to represent two positions into which the writing instructor can and inevitably does slip on various occasions. The first is the moral position, which is implicit in the rage to teach. It is but a small step from feeling that one has something valuable to impart to students to feeling that one is more valuable or, in some way, morally superior to one's students. In this instance, one's theoretical position, to the extent that it implicitly or explicitly asserts a value, may protect one from wounding at the hands of one's inferior students.

The second position I call the amoral or realist position. While the first sees itself as an attempt to move students from one moral position to another, the second asserts itself not as what ought to be but simply as what is. This is much more the position of the one who knows, and what one knows, to put the matter baldly, is reality. While the first position unconsciously presupposes a notion of autonomy that may be assumed by a particular self (there otherwise being no possibility of truly moral development), the latter does not. Rather the instructor is the reality he represents, and if students should appear to have some trouble grasping that reality, it must be because of something in the student that inhibits him or her from facing reality.

An instance of the first, or moral, position may be seen in Donna Qualley's *Turns of Thought,* and an instance of the second, in David Bartholomae's classic and powerful article "Inventing the University." In analyzing the works of these authors as instances of the positions I have described, I am in no way implying that anything either of these authors has to say about their respective subjects is wrong. I am in no position to assert that. I couldn't begin to elaborate a theory of critical thinking with the sophistication of Qualley. And I envy Bartholomae's article. It is very rare to find an article so clearly written that any intelligent reader may follow the argument and still find, as I do, upon returning to the article again and again, fresh insights hidden in its nooks and crannies. I analyze these articles only to show how the positions I have described might pro-

tect the instructor, who takes as his or her own the theories implicit
in these writings, from coming to a conscious awareness of narcissistic wounding by students.

The importance of this analysis is implicit in all I have said to
this point. If teachers of writing are to construct the writing class
as transitional environment, they must recognize students' subjectivities. They will be ill-positioned to do so unless they are able to
experience their own subjectivities as teachers. One manifestation
of this subjectivity is the experience of narcissistic wounding, of not
meeting a reality that affirms the self at its deepest levels. Such
wounding is not bad; rather from it one may develop as a person
and as a teacher. But in light of the power relation that exists between student and teacher, it may be very hard for teachers to admit that they have been hurt. And various theories of what the
teacher is supposed to do may furnish complicated rationalizations
for the unconscious experience of having been hurt.

Finally, the choice of these two theories is not an accident. They
are two of the defensive positions to which I am most prone. I have
been drawn to the notion of critical thinking, especially as it has appeared over the years in the liberatory pedagogy formulated by figures such as Henry Giroux, Ira Shore, and Paulo Friere. And, in this
way, I am an idealist of the kind Marx would disparage; I actually think
that changing how people think might change the world. There is
certainly an assumption of superiority in this belief. But paradoxically,
I am also a realist. I believe that changing people's minds and the way
they think may be about as hard as changing the economic structures.
But I said *about,* and for that reason, I, in moments of despair, sometimes think the best thing people can do is to change the way they
think so that they can better conform to reality. The tension between
these two positions evidences itself in my daily self-performance in
a sense of humor that tends toward the darkly pessimistic.

Donna Qualley and Self-Reflexivity

Qualley's pedagogy is directed toward cultivating in students self-
reflexive thought. She writes, "Reflexivity complicates our under-

standing and efforts to know by making us self-conscious, cognizant of our roles in the production of knowledge" (14). This sentence encapsulates themes I have developed at length. The understanding that reflexivity complicates I take to be the understanding of the intersubjective world of common sense. In the world of intersubjective common sense, one may easily become self-conscious when one, unknowingly or unthinkingly, violates one of the rules of the commonsense world. In the "spinach in one's teeth moment," one experiences oneself as standing out, as suddenly self-conscious, as embarrassed. At such a moment, one may experience oneself as distinct, in one's subjectivity, from one's role. In effect, Qualley's definition of reflexive thinking appears central to fourth-order consciousness.

Qualley quotes Elizabeth Minnich:

> [T]hinking reflexively is one of the grounds of human freedom, in part because it reveals to us that we are both subject and object of our own knowing, of our own culture, of our world. We are not just products, objects of our world, nor are we just subjects existing in a void. We are free subjects whose freedom is conditioned—not determined—by a world not of our own making but in many ways open to the effects of our actions. (14)

From the perspective of the daily world of common sense, the definition of freedom offered here is so ethereal as to be intangible. Freedom, in the commonsense realm, is more likely to be understood as freedom from want or freedom to want and buy anything. Only persons who are able however momentarily or transitorily to experience self-authorship are likely to experience this freedom. For surely self-authorship implies the capacity to regard one's subjective states as objects that in turn may shape one's sense of an objective world. Finally, and most significantly, Minnich—and one assumes Qualley—argues that the capacity to think reflexively is one of the grounds not just of freedom but of "human freedom."

Thinking reflexively seems to carry for Qualley a heavy moral freight. The capacity to reflect seems to make one human in a way that one who cannot think reflexively isn't. In effect, the teaching of reflexive thinking (and with it, the fourth order of consciousness) takes on the quality of a moral imperative. As I have indicated, I believe the move to the fourth order of consciousness does represent a developmental value. But a considerable difference is implied in whether one conceives of the teaching of this value as an ethical or a psychological enterprise. From my psychoanalytic perspective, Qualley's pedagogy appears largely ethical, and as a consequence, Qualley seems unable to recognize the psychological trials and tribulations students must undergo to move to reflexive thinking or critical thinking more generally.

Qualley writes, "To read essayistically means to approach a text with the conscious intention of engaging in a genuine dialogue with its ideas, a dialogue that may put the reader at risk because it can easily become a reflexive dialogue" (61). First, this definition of essayistic reading seems to presuppose what, from my psychoanalytic perspective, must first be developed: the "conscious intention of engaging in a genuine dialogue." If students are to do such a thing, they must first learn to extrospect. Only if the student is capable of entering into an extrospective relation with the text can he or she harbor the conscious intention of having a dialogue with it. And coming to an extrospective relationship with the text may prove difficult if the student has experienced destabilization during the reading experience. If that is the case, the student is more than likely to merge with the text, to assert relative to it a narcissistically infused interpretation (self-relation) that provides self-stabilization.

From my psychoanalytic perspective, Qualley has the process upside down. She locates a risk in reflexive thinking. This risk, she argues, following Brodkey, "involves learning, the modification (or risk of modification) of what's in your head as a result of your encounter with the text." This risk I believe does take place at first reading, though mostly unconsciously. The text is not something out there, and one's thoughts are not locked in one's head. When one reads, one's thoughts are modified. These modifications may act psychologically in one of two basic ways. They may affirm the reader in his or her sense of who he or she is and thus prove narcissistically stabilizing, or they may seem not to affirm the self of the reader and thus be experienced as destabilizing.

Failure of Self-Reflexivity or Argument for the Self?

Qualley analyzes in some detail the response of one student, Rob, to the educational writings of Paulo Freire. Through Rob's analysis, she illustrates why he fails to rise to reflexive thinking.

> When Rob announces at the outset of his first response that anyone who reads Freire's essay "can sit down and interpret it any way they desire," I already suspect that an authentic and (self)-critical dialogue is not likely to be forthcoming. If each reader is ascribed carte blanche to interpret text, then reading becomes *purely* a subjective activity, and any dialogue that could enlarge the reader's understanding becomes superfluous. (73)

I have received over the years a good number of papers that have started with the assertion, in one form or another, that one may read a text as one wishes or that everything is relative, isn't it. Like Qualley, I don't see such a beginning as necessarily a good sign of what is to follow. However, from my psychoanalytic perspective, I do not see this claim as the assertion of a subjectivist epistemology. I read it rather as a defensive assertion. As such it is an expression of the student's subjectivity, at a largely unconscious level, of his or her relation to the text and the larger classroom environment.

At a largely unconscious level, the student has responded psychologically to the text and to its presentation in the classroom environment. Moreover, this reading has destabilized the student. He or she then acts to restabilize the self through an interpretation that the student knows at a largely unconsciously level is not consonant with the presentation of the text in the classroom environment. The claim that anyone may interpret a text as he or she desires protects the student against attack on his or her deviant interpretation, one that stabilizes the self but also apparently puts it at odds with the classroom presentation of the text.

If students attempt to preserve themselves against attack, it might be because they have experienced themselves as attacked. The relativistic introduction represses a great deal that the student dare not say or even admit into consciousness. For example,

> I know you [the teacher] think Freire is hot stuff and has something to say or otherwise you probably wouldn't have assigned it. I, however, think what he has to say sucks. Everything he says and most of what you said in class too suggest to me that all of the education I had in high school was a waste of my time. I have been stuffed like a little birdie. Well, I wonder what Mr. Cranston, my favorite teacher, would have to say. He was a good guy and not a bird stuffer. As far as I am concerned, Freire is insulting Mr. Cranston. Don't get me wrong. I am not going to say any of this (mostly because I am not conscious of any of it). I am going to try to write your damn essay and I will "respond" to Freire but I am going to do it my way. Oh, and by the way, my father is a BANKER.

This response of my fictional Rob is intended to suggest that he might have experienced considerable narcissistic wounding from reading Friere and from the classroom presentation of Friere. Rob is forced to look back on his prior education and to conclude, since it did not encourage reflexive thinking, that there was something wrong with it. But to reject his previous education might involve also questioning the value he placed on his favorite teacher, Mr. Cranston. A deeper allegiance here, not to a system of education but to a person, is challenged. Surely, Rob's response to the banker model represents a gross misinterpretation of Friere, but the unconscious is not logical or rational. If Rob's father is a banker and if he respects that father, then Rob's father functions as a stabilizing selfobject. And from this perspective, whatever Friere might have intended, it's clear that he has little positive to say about banking.

The affective response of my narcissistically wounded fictional Rob is very close to rage. Suggesting to a teacher that the reading he or she has assigned stinks is very close to saying that the teacher stinks. The student cannot admit the rage into consciousness, however. Doing so would prove threatening to the student's selfobject relationship to the teacher and the overall classroom environment. Instead the student represses the rage and seeks self-stabilization through the construction of a subjective interpretation.

Qualley argues that in the real Rob's essay we find a form of interpretive clarity run amok because "Rob is arguing for a particular version of reality, not exploring one." And furthermore,

> Rob's concept of democratic dialogue—a rule designed to let everybody have his or her say—is vastly different from Freire's notion of a dialogue that leads to critical understanding. For Rob the dialogue of fraternity meetings seems to be more like a procedure that allows people to gain access to the floor so they can air their views and argue for what they already think. (74)

I would respond that, yes, of course, Rob is arguing for a reality, not exploring one. He is arguing, apparently, for the reality of his frat house and his fraternity meetings, as the selfobject that serves to restabilize him in the face of the narcissistic wounding he has experienced. Moreover and not accidentally, the form of dialogue for which Rob argues is the notion of dialogue that appears at the third order of consciousness. At this level, as Kegan suggests, people celebrate their subjectivity and the subjectivity of others. The procedures of the fraternity house, by allowing anyone to speak his mind if he wishes, allows for just that assertion and celebration of subjectivity.

The primary difficulty that I locate in Qualley is the assertion of reflexive thinking as a value and the teaching of it as a largely ethical enterprise directed at rational, ethical agents. Qualley notes, "[T]hat Rob curtails his inquiry prematurely may be the fault of a pedagogy (or a teacher) that does not nudge him hard enough to continue [in his explorations]" (74–75). If my analysis, however, is correct, it would take something more than a mere nudge—a very hard one indeed—to dislodge Rob from the reality that functions for him as a selfobject. And just imagine the difficulties if the real Rob resembled my fictional Rob. Nudging him might involve getting nudged back.

For Qualley the possibility of being nudged back, however, might not be readily apparent. Qualley infuses the type of thinking typical of the fourth order of consciousness with a strong moral charge. It is not likely for a person who enjoys this position relative to students to experience themselves as being nudged by a person who isn't, after all, at their level. Viewed in this way, the infusion of the fourth order of consciousness with a moral charge protects against any direct challenge to that order of thought. Psychoanalytically, if one assumes and asserts the fourth order of consciousness as a moral value, it may act as a stabilizing selfobject and as such serve as a form of psychological defense against the experience of narcissistic wounding. To put the matter baldly, the failure of students to assume one's moral position may illustrate primarily that students, in not rising to one's position, are demonstrating their moral inferiority.

Destabilization: Shame, Embarrassment, and Humiliation

I shift gears slightly to introduce three particularly painful psychological affects—shame, embarrassment, and humiliation—that play a significant role in the literature of self psychology. Self psychology concentrates not on guilt and the conflicts that it produces but on shame, humiliation, and embarrassment as affects that arise from the self's social embeddedness. Any one of these affects, either momentarily or more permanently and more deeply, may destabilize one's selfobject relations to the social world and thus destabilize the self. Qualley's concept of self-reflexiveness may be psychoanalytically understood as a selfobject that if taken up defensively, might neutralize these painful affects.

Qualley introduces the concept of reflexive thinking through a brief narrative of her move, at age twenty-two, to Australia to teach. Needing some plumbing supplies, she drove to a lumberyard but found it closed for a month. She then drove to a hardware store, but it did not have the parts she needed. The salesclerk said the correct parts could be ordered, but it would take a month to receive them because "most of their suppliers were closed between Christmas and the end of January." Qualley writes,

> I was stunned. Didn't they realize that if they kept their businesses open, the company would make more money?
>   The sales person seemed to read my thoughts. He looked at me and shrugged, "This ain't America, mate," he said, "we are not all bloody capitalists here." But I wasn't a capitalist, was I? Surely, it was just good business sense to want to make as much money as possible. (9)

On the basis of this experience and others like it, Qualley generalizes,

> If I really wanted to *understand* Australian culture and not simply judge it according to my American biases, I would have to call up and make the implicit and unconscious assumptions that I had acquired in my home country explicit. I would have to become *reflexive,* although I didn't know this at the time. (10, author's emphasis)

While she didn't know "this at the time," Qualley intends her narrative as an example of reflexive thinking and an argument for its potential value. The psychological need for this value (qua value) and thus how it may function as selfobject are implicit in the narrative. Qualley describes an experience of narcissistic wounding. I have experienced this wounding—this not being able to locate in the environment a response to my needs—simply by going to Home Depot. How much deeper, I must wonder, was Qualley's wounding?

Qualley's wounding, however, goes deeper than simple frustration. She stumbles into a situation replete with possibilities for shame and embarrassment and the powerful potentials in each for narcissistic wounding. And, indeed, the clerk, rather than helpfully attempting to explain to her the situation in a way more responsive to her particular self, implies that she is a capitalist. He uses her social ignorance against her. Qualley records, "But I wasn't a capitalist, was I? Surely, it was just good business sense to want to make as much money as possible." Qualley has been stereotyped; her particular experiential reality has been treated with indifference. Her self relative to her experiences as an American is momentarily, at least, destabilized.

Shame, embarrassment, humiliation, and the potential in these experiences for narcissistic wounding and self-destabilization are what I see in Qualley's narrative. But Qualley gives no hint about how she felt. Instead, she draws a lesson from her experience: "If I really wanted to understand Australian culture and not simply judge it according to my American biases, I would have to call up and make the implicit and unconscious assumptions that I had acquired in my home country explicit." But I have to wonder why Qualley felt the need not to judge, unless, in fact, she had felt a very powerful urge to do so, to condemn the other as other, in light of the wound she had received. And in her desire to "understand Australian culture"—why she should want to?—she projected out of her self the desire she had most felt in those alien environs: the desire to be understood. For one does have to wonder whether the Australian culture, for its part, felt any great desire to be understood by her. At the root then of Qualley's notion of reflexive thinking, I see a very powerful and understandable psychological motivation. If Qualley was to move out of her position of narcissistic vulnerability and to receive the understanding she needed as a particular self, it was necessary that she understand the Australian culture.

Not fitting in is not easy. In trying to do so, one inevitably fumbles the ball and flounders about. One is unable to pull it off with grace and aplomb. People see you sweat. Not fitting in is embarrassing and possibly humiliating. One may even feel ashamed. Taken in this context, the notion of reflexive thinking may be understood as an intellectual mechanism, a rationalization for and a repression of these disturbing affects. For some the mechanism may serve, more benignly, as a form of sublimation, a means by which one attempts to make intellectual profit from psychological destabilization. Affects are, after all, a way of learning.

If, however, one invests this notion with a moral freight, the possibility arises that one may, in one's pedagogy, create an intersubjective terrain between oneself and one's students that makes it difficult to see and acknowledge the affects that lie at the origins of that pedagogy. Shame, embarrassment, and humiliation—these are things students too may feel. The risk that arises from a conscious intention to engage in a genuine dialogue may be somewhat more palpable than simply having something changed in one's mind. It may mean experiencing shame and humiliation. One is ashamed, after all, more by what one does not know than by what one does. Embarrassment does not arise from having spinach between one's teeth; it arises when one is told that one does. One is embarrassed that one did not know. Students may feel this embarrassment a great deal. They didn't know, after all, that a comma wasn't supposed to go in this place and was supposed to go in that. And their embarrassment may run deeper if, in being asked to think reflexively, they find their self-images portrayed as limited, narrow, and ignorant.

One of course does not think of oneself as engaged in embarrassing or shaming students. One thinks instead that one is offering them a better way of thinking, one evocative of human freedom. The teacher offers them a value; if students can take up this value as selfobject, it might function as a form of sublimation for shame and embarrassment. I do not doubt that the notion of self-reflexive thinking embraced and taken up as a value may help stabilize some against embarrassment and shame. But I do very much doubt that students are likely to take up this notion as a value if the potentials for shame and embarrassment, implicit in the teaching of it, are not recognized and dealt with.

I am concerned in part with Qualley's theory as a manifestation of a possible broader trend in the field of composition studies. At times, at least, among proponents of critical thinking and cultural studies, I detect an evangelic tone. (For more of my thoughts on this subject, see Tingle, "Self.") Students, it seems, must be taught these things if they are to be saved from themselves and unshackled from their mind-forged manacles. Proponents of cultural studies are, of course, right. The media today have an unparalleled power; their capacity to shape not simply the agendas for thought and debate but the way people think and perceive their world is, in the Western world, unequalled in human history. Television is the true educator of the time. The question for me, then, is not whether media shape ideology and the way people think but how best and most effectively to indicate this fact to students.

David Bartholomae: Realist

Bartholomae's powerful "Inventing the University" concerns me in another way. It draws its power from the clarity with which it represents and evokes a deep-rooted psychological tendency. People seek out objects that are self-stabilizing. If these objects are in some way injured, so too is the person who takes them as selfobjects. One way to deal with such inevitable wounding, especially if it reverberates at the level of what Christopher Bollas calls the "unthought known" with an early traumatic experience of wounding, is to assert that the experience of such wounding is reality at root and bottom.

Bartholomae is such a realist and is not in the least concerned with the development of the individual. He is concerned, on the basis of the existing social order, with what is required of a student as he or she attempts to assume and master the "authority" of the academic voice. The authority of the academic voice, moreover, for Bartholomae is not a moral authority. The student struggles, Bartholomae says, to master an academic voice so that he or she might enter a "closed society." Bartholomae does not say this society is good or bad, only that entry into it allows one to speak with a certain recognizable authority. Bartholomae does refer to students, before they have mastered academic authority, as speaking with the "naïve codes of everyday life." The word *naïve* does not imply a moral lack, just ignorance.

Bartholomae writes, "It should be clear by now that when I think of 'knowledge' I think of it as situated in a discourse that constitutes knowledge in a particular discourse community, rather than as situated in mental 'knowledge sites.'" Bartholomae is not concerned, then, with individuals at all—as mental "knowledge sites"— and as such his term "naïve codes" does not represent a characterization of an individual's "mental knowledge site." Indeed, he is concerned only with knowledge as constructed by discourse. In this light, the discourse of "the naïve codes of everyday life" does not represent an inferior discourse, just one that is different from the discourse of the university.

In effect, Bartholomae describes as discourse the distinction between the third and fourth orders of consciousness. Students at the third order of consciousness, characterized by enmeshment in the intersubjective world of common sense, tend to employ in their writing, according to Bartholomae, "commonplaces." He writes,

> A "commonplace" then is a culturally or institutionally authorized concept or statement that carries with it its own elaboration. We all use commonplaces to orient ourselves in the world; they provide points of reference and a set of "pre-articulated" explanations readily available to organize and interpret experience. (138)

Commonplaces are truisms. They are the summing up of the wisdom of common sense. Because they carry with them—as prearticulated—their elaboration, the student who employs them feels no need to elaborate or qualify or explain the statement and thus is unable to move toward the academic voice, which is consistently marked by elaboration, qualification, and explanation.

Bartholomae does, however, locate in one student's writing on the prompt of creativity signs of the academic voice: "This writer is consistently and dramatically aware of herself forming something out of what has been said and out of what she has been saying in the act of writing" (154). In the word *forming,* especially in relation to what the author has been saying, one may detect signs of what Kegan calls self-authorship. The student appears dramatically aware of her self as self-authoring. However, this self, as Kegan asserts, is one that establishes itself and its autonomy only by breaking its relations to the world. Bartholomae, following Olson, seems to agree: "[T]he writer must learn that his authority is not established through his presence, but through his absence—through his ability, that is, to speak as a god-like source beyond the limitations of any particular social or historical moment" (155).

But while Kegan stresses the developmental rigors required— "separations of self" as he calls them—and while I have stressed throughout this chapter the potentials for self-destabilization entailed in such a move, Bartholomae appears to make light of the idea of self-development. We may, he says, call the move into the closed society "development," but that is because we are after all "teachers," or rather nice people, one supposes. Remarkably, though, for all his apparent disregard for development and the affective potentials that might attend it, Bartholomae is extremely attentive to the role of affect in students' writing. One student's failure to adequately generalize Bartholomae attributes to a failure of *courage*. Of another, he suggests the tactic of revision simply would not work because of the burden of conformity involved. Indeed, throughout his work, Bartholomae shows a deep and respectful awareness of the struggle students must undergo if they are to assume the authority of the academic voice.

Academic Writing: Becoming Someone One Is Not

While Bartholomae appears attentive to students' affective states and to the struggle involved in the movement to the academic voice, his socially informed notion of discourse is not consistent with a notion of psychological development. He is explicit on this point. In "Writing Assignments: Where Writing Begins," he writes, "To become like us, the student must, by writing, become like us. . . . The struggle of the student writer is not the struggle to bring out that which is within; it is the struggle to carry out those ritual activities that grant one entrance into a closed society" (300). The struggle, for Bartholomae, in other words, is not a psychological struggle but a social struggle to carry out ritual activities. Ultimately, the student writer "must become someone he is not."

Further, Bartholomae appears aware of the potential conse-
quences for the individual in this becoming someone one is not.
Arguing against a "too smooth" notion of writing as process, he
writes,

> If you think of other accounts [other than those of Flow-
> ers and Hayes] of the composing process—and I am think-
> ing of accounts as diverse as Richard Rodriguez's *Hunger*
> *or Memory* (1983) or Edward Said's *Beginnings* (1975)—
> you get a very different account of what happens when
> private motive enters into public discourse, when a per-
> sonal history becomes a public account. These accounts
> place the writer in a history that is not of the writer's own
> invention; and these are chronicles of loss, violence, and
> compromise. (142)

Part of the power of Bartholomae's article is that he makes no bones
about it. He does not sugarcoat the pill. The student's struggle to
move into the alien discourse of the university requires that he lose
himself. As a result, the chronicles of those who have made that
move are tales of loss, violence, and compromise. (See also Nancy
Welch's powerful response to Bartholomae in *Getting Restless,* 150.)

Bartholomae's representation of the move to the fourth order
of consciousness in ways confirms my own. As I have stressed, the
movement from one order to another involves students in self-destabilization and narcissistic wounding. Certainly for some, like Said
or Rodriguez, this wounding may prove intense, affecting them not
simply at the surface levels of self but far, far more deeply. Like
Bartholomae, I respect the student's struggle. But unlike him, I believe students deserve support if they attempt such a struggle. For
Bartholomae, from his perspective of social discourse, no such support is possible, since the self of the student is recognized only in
the affective by-products of the move from the discourse of common sense to academic discourse.

In effect, Bartholomae seems to conceive of the "closed society"
of academic discourse only as a source of narcissistic wounding and

self-fragmentation. If such is the case, then there is no way that the student may take up this closed society as a stabilizing selfobject or be supported, however momentarily, in the developmental movement enjoined by it. As Bartholomae argues, the student must, if he or she wishes to become one of "us," become what he is not. And so, also, teaching is not a matter of "drawing out" that which was within the self of the individual. Bartholomae's rejection of the notion of development may hinge in part on his conception of it.

The development of the self, as I understand it psychoanalytically, does not mean drawing out that which was within. The movement to the fourth order of consciousness does not mean a person is capable in some way of a truer or deeper experience of the self. It means only that she or he is capable, however momentarily and provisionally, of assuming a different relationship to the third order of consciousness and, accordingly to one's conception of knowledge, what it is and how it is conceived. Certainly learning how to make this move, as it is enjoined by the structures of the "closed society" of the university, can and does provoke narcissistic wounding. The purpose, however, of the psychoanalytic pedagogy and the writing class as transitional space is not to bring out the student's truer self but to afford a support that allows the student, as he or she undergoes destabilization, a restorative experience of the continuum of self.

The extreme social disjunctive that Bartholomae posits between the discourse of everyday life and the discourse of the academy does not seem to me psychologically accurate or, more precisely, psychologically healthful. I do not dispute that for some persons, the subjective experience of moving from the discourse of common sense to the discourse of the academy may be experienced as a disruption or disjunction in the continuum of self. But if this is the case, I would suggest the individual has taken up the "closed society" of the university in a way that acts to negate the possibility of further development. In effect, the person has taken up the university and the fourth order of consciousness as a negative selfobject, one that stabilizes the self in the face of the massive narcissistic wounding it has undergone at the cost of its very design. If this has been one's experience, then the movement into the closed society of the university does mean becoming someone one is not.

If one embraces the realist position as I define it, the only relation possible between student and teacher is a social relation. The teacher is defined as teacher only through his or her social relation to students; and students are students only in their social relation to teachers. If the student is to master the discourse of the teacher, the student must become what he or she is not: the teacher. Or as Bartholomae puts it: "If my students are going to write for me by knowing who I am—and if this means more than knowing my prejudices or psyching me out—it means knowing what I know; it means having the knowledge of a professor of English" (140).

Conformity and Mimicry

But how does one learn what the professor knows, so that one can become not a student? By attempting, apparently, to make one's social role as student conform as much as possible to the social role of the teacher, through mimicry or imitation. Bartholomae writes,

> It may very well be that some students will need to learn to crudely mimic the "distinctive register" of academic discourse before they are prepared to actually and legitimately do the work of the discourse, and before they are sophisticated enough with the refinements of tone to do it with grace or elegance. To say this, however, is to say that our students must be our students. (162)

In effect, students are marked as students by their necessary inability adequately to mimic those persons who define them as students, their teachers.

I know of course what Bartholomae is writing about. Any teacher who has had a student come to the office and say "What do you want?" knows what Bartholomae is writing about. If one follows Bartholomae, the only honest answer would be, "Well, I want you to be me. I want you to know what I, as the teacher, know." That is indeed what one wants; maybe not precisely that the student know what the teacher knows but, more precisely, how the teacher, operating at the fourth order of consciousness, knows. But if the student knew that, if he or she knew about self-authorship, it is unlikely he or she would be there in the office asking, "What do you want?"

One finds oneself in an existential impasse. And it is no good at all to pretend this impasse is not present or that the social dimension of the student-teacher relationship does not exist. It does exist, and it produces sometimes students who move into the closed society of the university. Most frequently, however, it produces mangled prose or, more precisely, prose in which the teacher sees himself and his thoughts reflected back to him as in a fun house mirror. That the social relationship between student and teacher works in ways that all teachers of writing have surely come to know, however, should not lead one to conclude that it is the only possible relationship between student and teachers.

Instructors' theories may function as stabilizing selfobjects. Admittedly, Bartholomae's theory, with its emphasis on struggle and even on explosively becoming someone one is not, might seem to some a curiously unstabilizing selfobject. But Bartholomae's perspective may ultimately prove stabilizing, at least for some, because it makes wounding and struggle simply part of the order of things, especially the social order of things. Indeed, Bartholomae's theory of the social seems very much one of the existential kind. The teacher and the student work in a kind of no-exit situation. Anxiety and struggle and wounding and falseness are simply part of the scene. If one is a realist, these are what one sees. If one can't see them, then perhaps one is a student or maybe just not tough enough. No one ever said being an existential hero was easy.

One's theory of writing, as selfobject, not only stabilizes the instructor subjectively but also informs his or her activity as instructor. And in light of the teacher's position of power, students inevitably respond to the teacher's activities. A narcissistic circuit, a kind of unconscious fusion between instructor and students, builds up, making it difficult for the instructor to recognize the individual selves of students. The generalized anxiety and struggle that Bartholomae, for example, locates in students' attempt to enter the closed society of the university block out the fact that different selves will experience and deal with the demands of the social situation in different psychological ways.

Bartholomae suggests, for example, that students start to invent themselves as literary critics through an act of appropriation. He writes, "They begin [to be invented as literary critics] with a moment of appropriation, a moment when they can offer up a sentence that is not theirs, as though it were their own" (145). Bartholomae is not concerned with what might push a student to such an act of appropriation. He wishes just to describe what is necessary—this act of appropriation—if students are to invent themselves as literary critics. Consequently, the whole issue of the student's relation (what might motivate him or her) to the act of appropriation and whether it involves students in an experience of falseness does not arise.

For me, however, it did arise in the course of my personal development as a student. As for Bartholomae, he writes, "I can remember when, as a graduate student, I would begin papers by sitting down to write literally in the voice—with the syntax and vocabulary—of the strongest teacher I had met" ("Inventing" 145). This imitation, however, was something that I, especially as an undergraduate, had a great deal of difficulty doing. I could not mimic. I recollect, in fact, having a friend, the son of a literature professor, visit me in the stacks. Surrounded by piles of books, I was scribbling feverishly away. My friend asked me what I was doing and I told him. He said, "Look, Nick, they are not interested in the truth. All they want is a gracefully written essay."

From one perspective, my friend gave me very good advice. I sensed that at the time and even tried to listen to it. But I seemed constitutionally unable to approach the writing task that way. Writing was for me at that time not simply a matter of style or of mastering certain discourse conventions but a confrontation or encounter with new ideas, theories, perceptions, subjectivities, and outlooks. I wasn't interested just in talking the talk or walking the walk. Perhaps at the time, I felt, naïvely no doubt, that I was in search of the truth. Looking back, I would now say that, for whatever reason, I found it very important to somehow assert and locate the truth of my self-relation to the topic. Just analyzing the assignment and writing gracefully in response was beyond me. I spent inordinate amounts of time twisting the assignment around and doing background work, hoping that I could make it conform to something I wished to understand.

I am not comparing the way I wrote as an undergraduate with the way Bartholomae wrote as a graduate student to prove anything. My point is far more minimal. I only suggest that we responded to the social pressure in the situation in different ways. Bartholomae could mimic at a relatively conscious level. Whether he could do it easily, I don't know, though his awareness of the struggle involved in mastering academic discourse suggests it wasn't easy. Perhaps because the social pressures exerted by the environment were so intense, I could not mimic, at least consciously. I stuck with and insisted on establishing my particular and idiosyncratic self-relation to the educational environments.

On the basis of this conscious awareness, I am inclined to analyze students' difficulties with mastering discourse conventions in a different way. Perhaps the problem does not lie so much in attempting to move into a discourse as in moving away from the discourse of common sense. The act of appropriation, as Bartholomae puts it, central to the move into academic discourse is, if one thinks about it, a rather strange act. It is "a moment when they [students] can offer up a sentence that is not theirs, as though it were their own" (145). This formula might appear to be one for plagiarism, but of course it isn't. It is rather the moment when one narcissistically fuses with (in a blurring of self and object) and takes up as selfobject the discourse of academia. And if taking up this discourse as selfobject also means a movement, implicit and potential at least, into the fourth order of consciousness, one must undergo a complete revision of one's relations to previously maintained (and maintaining) intellectual selfobjects.

*True and False Selves: The Capacity
to Conform as Self-Development*

Taking up the discourse of academia may be hard for some because it may involve being or becoming false or inauthentic in relation to the language one has spoken. This language, moreover, has been, as the language of common sense and commonplaces, the very language that functioned as one's connective tissue to and with the social sphere and one's family. The commonplaces of one's social group and one's family function as a slang, a language central to one's social placement and in the recognition of the self relative to that placement. The whole point of a commonplace is that it does not require elaboration and qualification. Rather if it is spoken to a member of one's group, one may be assured that the other will understand, and if the other does not but requires elaboration, he or she is not a member of one's social group.

Encouraging students to remove the "I" from their writing and to become aware of things called "clichés" (and not to use them) are ways of trying to suggest to students what academic discourse is and isn't. But much more is involved here, for the student who might attempt to respond to such encouragement, than simply making a rhetorical move. Psychologically, the attempt to respond to this encouragement may involve students in experiences of destabilization, falseness, inauthenticity, and even betrayal of the language that they have spoken and that continues to bind them to their significant selfobjects. Language as commonplace narcissistically fuses and binds one to one's social group; as such it is aimed not at saying more but at saying as little as possible about the distinctness or ultimate otherness of either speaker.

Commonplaces in student writing act as forms of stabilizing selfobjects. They assume and assert one's position within a particular group. The authority assumed and asserted, from the fourth order of consciousness, through the commonplace, however, appears bogus exactly because it assumes a group affiliation and does not appear an assertion of self-authorship. In self-authorship, putatively at least, one cannot assume the other is a member of one's group, especially if one is a student. Students shouldn't therefore and most frequently don't use slang because that's a signal that one is a student. Self-authorship requires that one be conscious about oneself as writer or speaker. One writes, as Bartholomae notes, in a way that suggests one is aware of writing. One qualifies, elaborates, asserts assumptions, demonstrates logic, and supplies evidence. One knows that "for example" is not proof.

For some this consciousness of oneself as speaker can be downright paralyzing. The result amounts to performance anxiety. For others like me, the effort to perform self-authorship may lead to a struggle with the self, with an attempt, as one assumes the language or discourse conventions, to find and establish the truth of one's relation to what is being said. For some, given the break that must occur with one's commonplaces, this effort, the very action, may lead the writer to feel that he or she is being not true to the self but inauthentic and false. And if this is the case, then as Bartholomae puts it, moving into academic discourse may indeed be experienced as becoming someone one is not.

Because of my particular psychoanalytic view, however, I simply do not believe that one becomes someone one is not. And the very attempt to become someone one is not, as enjoined by the conventions of self-authorship, necessarily has psychological repercussions. As an example of such possible repercussions, I offer a peculiar student writing. I call it peculiar in part because the circumstances surrounding its writing were peculiar.

I took over a class in the third week of the quarter. The students had already begun their first paper; I introduced myself and asked them to change gears a bit on the papers they were writing. In the end, I received one that started out very much feeling like an "A" paper on the topic of obedience to authority. It was a bit on the thin side but clever. This part, I soon realized, had been written largely for the assignment of the previous instructor. I saw at the bottom of the page another part that had been written for me.

> Can you believe this paper? Though it is written in train
> of thought, it has structure, new paragraphs for each new

idea and topic sentences. The paper has an introduction, a progression throughout the body and a conclusion. I wrote it for someone who would analyze everything about this paper but the true depth of thought behind it. I wrote this for a Writing professor.

As I read back over this paper, I am embarrassed of it. Being the perfect little intelligent blond girl all my life has produced in me the almost unconscious skill of kissing ass. You can see it in the way I write, do assignments and generally interact with my "superiors," most often teachers. I think it has something to do with my innate selfishness and self-centeredness. I want certain things for myself in life (or have been brought up by society from an early age to want certain things for myself), and through experience have found that acting and performing in a kiss ass manner will get me what I want. To me, it is almost like using people has become an art. Is that my fault for being weak or society's fault for producing such experiences? I don't know. I just don't.

The one thing that I really worry about now is not that I am being unoriginal, but that I am being unoriginal in order to reach a goal that may not be what I truly want. I need to decide what I want to do with my life, to have a true goal to reach for. At this point, I am just sick of doing things for reasons that I am not even sure of. I want to lead a happy life in pursuit of goals that fulfill me. That, in a nutshell, is my main struggle with the influence of others.

This paper, overall, is a little anomalous. It doesn't offer a picture of a student struggling to master, in mangled prose, self-authorship. Rather, as I indicated, this student seems very close to having mastered, at least at the level of discourse, some of the basic elements of academic writing. Of course one would not be likely to come across a testimony of this kind from a student who was struggling to master academic discourse. Rather, this student's conviction, based on her experience, that she can write academically is what allows her to express her true feelings in what she wrote to me. I say "true feelings" because I believe strongly that instructors construct students' responses. And I take seriously this student's perception of her ability to please the teacher. Perhaps, unconsciously, she had felt my desire that she express the truth of her relationship to the topic, and in expressing her "true feelings" was attempting once again to please the teacher.

But this possibility admitted, I think the student's writing does offer at least a glimpse into the potentials for narcissistic wounding that may occur when students experience themselves as conforming to or appropriating the language of the "writing professor." This student seems to perceive the writing professor as a person interested only in the craft of the utterance, in such things as thesis statements, topic sentences, beginning, middle, and end. This interest she felt she had followed in the first part of the paper, and I had been convinced enough that I, as a writing professor, felt the first part was close to the "A" level. But reading back over the paper, the student feels "embarrassed of it."

Whence this embarrassment? I believe I in part produced it by shifting, in accord with my theory, the intersubjective terrain between student and teacher. Had I not appeared and asked students to write for me more from the position of their selves, this particular piece of writing might not have appeared. But it appears that this piece of writing is only the tip of the iceberg. The student writes, "Being the perfect little intelligent blond girl all my life has produced in me the almost unconscious skill of kissing ass." The piece of writing that embarrassed the student appears part and parcel of an ongoing self-struggle she, "the perfect little intelligent blond girl," has experienced for some time.

The embarrassment seems to arise from the student's sense that having written in the way she wrote for the writing professor parallels the way she has presented herself (or been perhaps perceived) as the "perfect little intelligent blond girl." The "perfect little blond girl" is not she; and the paper perfectly crafted for the instructor does not represent the "true depth of her thought." I am not sure whether the part of the paper written for me is intended to represent the true depth of her thought, but it does indicate that she does not believe she is a "perfect little intelligent blond girl." No, she accuses herself of being an innately selfish, self-centered user of others and a "kiss ass." This very strong negative characterization suggests that the student may have felt something stronger than embarrassment, something approximating a profound sense of personal shame, upon rereading what she had written.

Shame, humiliation, and embarrassment—these affects are very much associated, in the psychoanalytic literature, with narcissistic wounding and injury. One may be ashamed or embarrassed, as in the example of Qualley, by being true to one's unconscious assumptions and then being brought up short, to a painful awareness of one's limitations, by a reality that does not respond to one's truth. Or one may feel ashamed not of one's limitations but of one's narcissistic powers if they bring rewards and acknowledgement that are not, in fact, expressions of one's true self. This shame is of the sort one may feel at being proclaimed a hero when one did not and does not experience oneself as heroic.

Shame is very much an intersubjective experience. As a result, the narcissistic destabilization produced by it may operate in not one but two directions. One may feel ashamed of oneself for taking credit for accomplishments that are not the result of the assertion of one's true self. One may also feel ashamed of the other, especially if this other is taken as superior, for imputing to one a virtue one does not experience oneself as having and does not affirm the self, consequently, in its design. The student hints at the possibility of this complex experience when she writes, "To me, it is almost like using people has become an art. Is that my fault for being weak or society's fault for producing such experiences? I don't know. I just don't." Of whom or what precisely am I ashamed? the student seems to ask. Of myself, because I am weak and yield to the power to please at a loss of myself? Or of society ("my superiors") who are so easily deceived by me?

The question that the student asks is, at the psychological level, real. There is and can be no fixed answer to it. Rather each individual will or won't answer it in his or her particular way in the course of

his or her development. D. W. Winnicott argues that the conflict between the true and the false self (the self necessary for "conformity")
may be particularly powerful in adolescents. This conflict is potent
in part because implicit in it is the growing disillusionment of the
adolescent with the values, philosophies, and outlooks of her superiors. The student asks her question—about whether she is the problem or whether society is—because she wants to know who is at fault.
In its overall thrust, her testimony suggests that she is finding society more and more to be the culprit. This faultfinding is itself part of
the process of disillusionment and is necessarily self-destabilizing.

I in no way suggest that either the first writing assignment or
the way I changed it was the direct and sufficient cause of the student's destabilization. I don't know what this student's real crisis was;
I suspect she was involved, at that early stage of her academic career, in trying to decide what exactly she wanted to do with her life
and, in relation to that, her education. In effect, the two parts of the
paper may have represented an acting out of this much deeper crisis. But my main point still stands. Students bring their selves into
the writing class. The developmental move enjoined of them, the
tasks we ask them to do, involve students in their selves in ways that
may occasionally reverberate to the deeper levels of their psyches.
When students attempt to master academic discourse, something
far more complex is going on than can be captured in the idea of
becoming someone one is not.

Academic Writing and the Ideology of Self-Denial

I have to wonder how many students experience the writing professor as a person interested only in how one says something (academically) and not at all in what a person truly thinks. If the answer is "many," I have also to wonder how many students might
experience themselves, sometimes consciously but mostly unconsciously, as being false to their true selves when they write for the
writing professor. And I have to wonder too whether, if this particular experience is not somehow at the root of the perception, it would
seem, at least of a substantial number of students, that learning to

write academically means learning how to "bull" or, less politely, BS. I have asked students what they mean by "bull" and have received no satisfactory answer. Perhaps I catch them off guard when I ask, especially since I really am asking. But overall, it seems to mean "writing something I don't believe and don't care about and certainly don't understand in a language that can convince another (the teacher or the teaching assistant) that I do believe, care, and understand."

If that is the definition of "bull," I have to wonder whether the mangled prose, or "engfish," as Ken Macrorie called it, that one occasionally receives is the result not so much of seeing oneself crudely mimicked as it is of the student being false. Being false is not, of course, necessarily bad if one does it convincingly and obtains from the doing what one wants relative to one's true self. But a question arises: Does academic writing necessarily require that one be untrue to the self? Bartholomae would seem to say so, and Patricia Williams seems to agree when she writes,

> What is "impersonal" writing but denial of self? If withholding is an ideology worth teaching, we should be clearer about that as the bottom line of the enterprise. We should also acknowledge the extent to which denial of one's authority in authorship is not the same as the elimination of oneself: it is a ruse, not reality. And the object of such a ruse is to empower still further. (268)

Williams, like Bartholomae, writes as one who has been through the system and who has mastered impersonal writing. Unlike Bartholomae, however, she suggests that mastering discourse is a matter not of becoming someone one is not but of "denying the self." Further, if I read her correctly, because the self is denied along with the authority of that self as self, impersonal writing is experienced as a ruse, a kind of fakery, not a reality. The object of this falseness is empowerment or, more nakedly, power.

But power can be and is frequently narcissistically sustaining. As a teacher or any person of authority, one has the right to speak by virtue of that authority alone. But the problem is, from a psychological point of view, that while this power may sustain the self at one level, at another it is a ruse or denial of the self. One has the right to speak, but as impersonal authority, one is spoken (by one's discourse) as teacher, policeperson, or judge. This is a painful paradox, one recognized as such especially by the student, the speeder, and the criminal. It is perhaps a paradox conducive to social order, but it is not one conducive to education or psychological self-development. Williams puts it in a different way:

> In a vacuum I suppose there's nothing wrong with this attempt to empower; it generates respect and distance and a certain obeisance to the sleekness of a product that has been skinned of its personalized complications. But in a world of real others, the cost of such exclusive forms of discourse is empowerment at the expense of one's relations to those others; empowerment without communion. (268)

"Bull" is not so much a reality as it is an experience of oneself relative to the act of speaking. As such, it is ubiquitous. Students are not the only ones who experience it. I am aware that what I write is not something that my relatives would understand. One relative did attempt to read something I had written in the academic manner. He said of course that he was proud that I had published something, and then he indicated that what he had read seemed mighty "wordy" and wondered if it might have been put in fewer words. I have heard exactly these words from students when I asked them to read something difficult, and it is easy to feel, in this instance, that "this is too wordy" is code for "I don't like it" or "it has no earthly use that I can imagine."

I don't believe that one must become someone one is not to enter academic discourse. I don't believe it because I believe in the unconscious. The roots of oneself are there in one's most elemental design. And part and parcel of that elemental design are one's most primordial selfobjects, one's parents, one's relatives, one's earliest social situations. When one writes, even academically, one writes in relation not to a single audience but in relation to multiple audiences. One is not even aware of some of these audiences, though those early and most primordial audiences may be the very ones that shape one's expectations and anticipations relative to the audience one more consciously addresses. My relative's "wordy" comment, though I tried to dismiss it as the opinion of a person for whom literature is *People Magazine,* nonetheless hurt. Even admitting that it hurt was hard. But in doing so, I have come to wonder whether one of the audiences for whom I write may not be my relatives. No wonder, then, at moments when I write academically, I experience what I have written as incomprehensible, unintelligible, and of no earthly use.

Fundamentally, elementally, and basically, one wants to be recognized. This need is at the very heart of the narcissism, the desire, the yearning, and perhaps the longing for an affirmation of oneself in its activity. The experience, the sense that one is or has been active is not something one can pump up in oneself; it requires for its realization the recognition of another. Recognition and empathy are central to what the psychoanalyst Jessica Benjamin calls the intersubjective view of the self and its development.

> A person comes to feel that "I am the doer who does, I am the author of my acts," by being with another person who recognizes her acts, her feelings, her intentions, her existence, her independence. Recognition is the essential response, the constant companion of assertion. The subject declares "I am, I do," and then waits for a response, "You are, you have done." (21)

The very possibility of the experience of oneself as independent, as the author of one's acts, or of being, as Kohut puts it, an independent center of initiative depends upon the possibility of having one's acts recognized by another.

I did not, however, feel recognized, not in the way I would most fully have liked, by my relative's response. Of course, in trying to read what I had written at all—though I doubt he read much—he did recognize my activity, and I might have rested content with that alone. But when one writes, one wants to be understood, to be taken as having at least said something and not as just having produced a plague of "wordiness." In that way, I did not feel recognized in my intentions, in my meanings, and in my subjectivity. My point of course is that in writing academically, one may be making a significant psychological move. One may begin to express oneself in a way that is not intelligible or comprehensible to those audiences most deeply embedded in oneself. If that is the case, one may indeed be cutting oneself off from those audiences whose recognition would be, above all others, of the greatest importance.

If one really is cutting oneself off from one's audience, writing academically for the one who knows how and perhaps most especially for the one who is trying to learn how may be experienced as pouring good money after bad. One is trying to learn to write and to think in a way (to gain entry to that closed society) that cuts one off exactly from those audiences from which one most desires recognition. No wonder students become enervated. No wonder they write things they don't understand and don't care about. The psychological roots of BS run very deep. No wonder some might experience themselves as becoming someone they are not.

One may of course receive enormous narcissistic gratification by moving into and mastering a particular mode of discourse. At the simplest level, one may experience oneself, for example, as particularly intelligent. Additionally, one may be rewarded by the applause of one's peers, by promotions, and by recognition as a specialist or "expert" knower in a certain area of knowledge construction. One finds one's activities as expert knower recognized by the discourse terrain in which one operates. I am not concerned here with the overall effects of this narcissistically informed identification of the individual with his or her discourse terrain. But I am concerned with the effects of such identification on students who are attempting to enter the fourth order of consciousness.

My central point in my analysis of Qualley and Bartholomae has been this: I do not argue with or in any way dispute their claims about critical thinking or mastering academic discourse. I have learned important things about each from both. I have wanted instead to point to the narcissistic investment of each in the theories or ways of thinking they represent. In both cases, it seems to me, the nature of this investment makes it difficult not simply to see but even to conceive of the psychological implications for the self of either position. Indeed, the word *discourse* seems necessarily to void even the presence of a self in it. The word *discourse* is designed to evoke not self-expression but rather its opposite, whatever that might be. The idea of discourse as self-expression misses the boat. But to the extent that discourse acts, rhetorically, to obliterate the self, it also necessarily fails to recognize that the mastery of discourse or critical thinking requires that students develop, if they are to take up either as a selfobject, a psychological or self-relation to it.

Neither perspective recognizes the developmental challenge enjoined by the university. They cannot see the narcissistic destabilization necessarily entailed by that move, nor are they positioned to use students' vital narcissism to assist them in that move. The self wants to develop, and the fuel of that development is narcissism. Or more precisely, the self must develop if it is not to remain a victim of its relatively archaic and grandiose narcissism. If it does not develop relative to its particular design and the potentials of its immediate circumstances, it will remain prone to excessive fragmentation. Its world will simply not recognize it. If one is to develop, then, one must take up different selfobjects, those that affirm one's design and afford potentials for recognition.

One such selfobject might be, in its broadest parameters, the fourth order of consciousness. Or it might be a car, or the yearning to make a million dollars. The university, however, is not in the business of selling cars, nor can it guarantee anyone a million dollars. What it has to teach or to give as a possible stabilizing selfobject is a particular way of thinking about the world and one's relationships to it. I am convinced that this particular way of thinking has an inherent value for the individual. Coming to think in this particular way represents not a loss of self but, at the level of ideation and intellect, the experience of self-authorship, or as Qualley puts it, freedom of a particularly human kind. The good the university has to give is a great good, one that can nourish the individual and may even encourage a particular moral development.

Some few students will, in relation to their psychological needs or psychological configuration, come to recognize this good and seek it out. But this only means that at present, the university and higher education in general do not educate but simply act as a filtering system by which to locate those persons who might perpetuate its institutions. This situation is simply not enough. The challenges that face the present generation of students are enormous. They are not simply individual financial challenges, either; they are, indeed, challenges to the very economic, social, and political institutions that make possible the idea of an individual financial challenge. The university must do a better job, a much better job of assisting students in their self-development. This issue is not ethical but practical: the attempt to afford students a selfobject, a way of thinking, that allows them to make sense of and find meaning in a world changing right before their eyes.

For those who believe it, this task might appear, and perhaps is, daunting. But the writing class as transitional environment is a place to start.

4 / The Transitional Environment and Intersubjectivity

Here I offer a narrative of a particular writing assignment to suggest what the writing class as transitional environment might feel like. I am reluctant to offer anything more definitive than an impression, because I don't want to suggest there are certain rules, procedures, or methodologies for the construction of such an environment. Many instructors of writing already know a good deal about this environment. But if that knowledge remains relatively unthought, it may be partly because of the widespread belief that the writing instructor must always be doing something rather than being something.

What the writing instructor most needs to *be*, of course, is him- or herself. I do not mean that in his or her various "doings," the writing instructor is not being him- or herself. I am simply warning against the idea that the writing class as transitional environment can be constructed by following certain rules. According to Winnicott, there is a kind of doing that emanates from being. He calls it creativity and places it in opposition to the other kind of doing—rule-responsive doing—which he calls "reactive-doing." This latter form of doing is something everyone must, in his or her development, learn how to do. It is the sort of doing that is absolutely necessary for fitting in with or adjusting to the dictates of the reality principle.

There is not just one reality principle; every person has internalized in the course of his or her development his or her own highly subjective version of it. But if a person, Winnicott suggests, is always experiencing his or her self as responding only reactively to the reality principle, she or he loses all sense of inward vitality. Life becomes one damn thing after another. Thus the critical importance of the doing that comes from being. Living creatively—having the experience of it—is the same as living vitally. In a creative relation to the real, one is able to experience oneself again in one's subjectivity. And in that experience, one is in contact, however momentarily and largely unconsciously, with one's infant self, with that brief time during which one experienced oneself as the creator of the world (*Home* 39–54).

I am reluctant then to set down procedures for the construction of the writing class as transitional environment because I don't want to give the impression that constructing it is a matter of doing something and not a matter of being something. I could state that as a rule, I suppose, but my particular self-image will simply not allow me to be fatuous Polonius to the groaning Hamlet. But more significant than the idiosyncrasies of my narcissism is the idea that if one is able to establish a creative relationship with all the things that must be done, one may also assist one's students in doing the same. Their narcissism, their sense of being the creators of the world, must be engaged if they are to establish new and self-created relations to the developmental move in which they are involved.

Teaching Epictetus?

The assignment that I analyze here was developed for the third unit of the previously discussed Writing 2. This unit was to be devoted to the humanities, and I decided to have my students read *The Enchiridion* by Epictetus. Why Epictetus, a minor Stoic who philosophized around the time of Marcus Aurelius? The choice may seem eccentric, and indeed I suppose it was. My brother was going through a divorce and happened to mention he had been reading *The Enchiridion* and had found in it some relief. I downloaded a copy from the Web and read it initially as a way of trying better to understand what my brother was experiencing at the time.

I was surprised by the clarity of what I read. While I am no expert on Stoicism, the work seemed to offer the fundamentals of that position in a straightforward way. It also told me a little about Roman life and how to properly comport oneself at the baths. I was also interested, in a general way, by the fact that Epictetus had been born a slave. Here was Stoicism arising at the other end of the social pole from figures like Marcus Aurelius and Seneca. What was the connection, I wondered—or was it a matter of that vague thing, the zeitgeist—between an emperor and a slave that should have led them to espouse a similar philosophy? Or was Stoicism, as Nietzsche might have it, a slave philosophy? These thoughts piqued my imagination and afforded material for speculative reverie.

I liked the idea of assigning Epictetus to students in part because of the way he wrote. Actually, he did not write; his oral ruminations were taken down by his followers in a far from systematic form. His thought appeared in chunks, some no more than a paragraph long, on this topic or that, but it all boiled down to an attempt to say what Stoicism might be and what might be entailed of the individual were he or she to pursue Stoicism as a way of life. I liked the chunks. I thought they might relieve students of the effort to master and recapitulate an entire systematic argument. *Relieve* is perhaps not the right word. Rather I hoped the brevity of the chunks might inhabit students' attempts simply to recapitulate what Epictetus had said.

Students' desire to demonstrate in writing that they have understood a reading is very strong. This tendency, moreover, is encouraged in the bulk of their general education classes, where recapitulation or, as students say, regurgitation is all. But unless they were able to dig deeply into Epictetus's first principles and then arrange a series of chunks in logical order, Epictetus's work would not afford enough "knowledge bits" to fill the five-page paper I wanted. I hoped the chunks would provide a different sort of reading experience, that they might, with their metaphors, similes, analogues, and occasional aphorisms, offer matter for rumination. Students simply don't read enough this way. First, they are usually given far too much to read, and second, they are too frequently given it in textbook form.

But if the chunks worked in the way I hoped they would, students might, through rumination, come to form more or less conscious subjective relations to the material. This was my overall hope: that students might experience the reading of Epictetus as in some way transformative and that in their writings they might articulate the nature of this transformation. To develop a space where such subjective responses might appear acceptable, I told the students how I had come across Epictetus and why I had decided to assign him. I wanted my selection to appear to the students not arbitrary, certainly, but at least idiosyncratic. I wanted to suggest that if my relation to Epictetus was idiosyncratic, so might theirs be. To this end, too, I tried to use the word *Stoic* as little as possible. I didn't want the students to take Epictetus as representative of the Stoic philosophy and read through Epictetus's words toward some abstract notion of Stoicism.

The Shaping Power of the Instructor

In working on what I call the "presentation" of the material, I attempted to offer the work of Epictetus as something that had not been preinterpreted by me, the instructor. I agree with Lad Tobin when he writes,

> Many writing teachers deny their tremendous authority in the classroom because it does not fit the image they would like to project. Most of us are uncomfortable admitting that we are the center of a "decentered" classroom, that we hold so much power, that we are largely responsible for success, and, even worse, for failure. (20)

Teachers do have tremendous authority, especially in shaping the way students understand what they are to read and to write on. The way the teacher presents or, perhaps more precisely, "embodies" the material can greatly determine how and whether students are able to respond to it subjectively.

I observed, for example, a class in which the instructor delivered a lucid exposition of an article about social conformity. The instructor was attempting to make sure students understood the assumptions and argument implicit in the article. These were things students would have to know for their upcoming writing assignment. Toward the close of the presentation, the instructor attempted to elicit a slightly less directed form of discussion by asking his students whether they had found anything troubling in the analysis he had just delivered. The students, speaking almost as one, said no. The article was perfectly clear. Human beings were social creatures; all they learn they learn from their socialization. As such, human beings are herd animals, who have no thoughts of their own, and who simply do what those around them do.

This conclusion about the nature of the human beast students found, with a rather calm complacency and faint air of cynical world-weariness, in no way troubling. I don't believe this apparent acceptance was actually the case; more than a few students in that room found this depiction of the human beast troubling, though largely at an unconscious level. Students' access to this troubled feeling, though, had in large part been cut off by the instructor's presentation of the materials.

The instructor was acting responsibly, of course. He was not trying to repress or inhibit his students; he was instead trying to help, to show them the key concepts and how they fit together. But in doing so, he was cut off from any access to how students might understand. How they understood, in this instance and relative to his presentation, was how he the instructor understood. The result was a narcissistic mirroring of student and teacher, with the paradoxical result that the instructor finally appeared somewhat troubled by his students' world-weary cynicism.

The authority or power of the instructor, as the one who knows in relation to such matters as intellection, ideation, and the general making of meaning, is indeed very great. The creation of the writing class as transitional environment does not in any way represent an attempt to abrogate or deny that power. If anything, my construction of the writing class as transitional environment represents an attempt fully to acknowledge that power and its possible effects on the student as learner and person. When students step into my class-

room, they willy-nilly step into my subjectivity and become en-
meshed in it. I am at the center of things. The question, for me, as
the person at the center of things, is how my authority may act to
direct, determine, and inhibit students' subjective responses.

A. Bronson Alcott wrote, "The true teacher defends the student
against his own influence" (qtd. in Gardner 3). I take this somewhat
slippery statement to mean that "true" teachers do their very best
to protect their students from the teachers' influence. In effect, I
would like to use my authority as a teacher in a way that keeps students from being influenced by it. I know, however, that while I may
take Bronson's statement as an ideal, it is strictly impossible to
achieve. I find it remarkable, for instance, that only once, in the four
or five times that I have required students to read Epictetus, did a
student ask why I had assigned such a thing. Instead, it seems that
students assume if a teacher assigns it, there must be some sort of
reason for it. Perhaps *reason* is too strong a word. Maybe it was simply sufficient that I as the authority assigned it. If we are truly to
cultivate critical thinking, we need to assist students in becoming
more critical somehow of teachers and their authority.

Shaping as Self-Exploration

Because I am aware of the powerfully determinative effects of my
presentation on students' understanding, I in part envision my various assignments as mini or micro experiments. I form, on the basis
of my psychoanalytic understanding, a hypothesis about the potential problems and influences of an assignment, and I try to ascer-
tain how students respond to it. In one assignment, I experimented
and made a mistake. I had good reasons for assigning the reading. I
taught a writing class linked with an introduction to ethics and
wanted somehow to impress on students that ethical decisions are
part of our daily lives and do not revolve around such distant hot
topics as abortion, euthanasia, and capital punishment.

Only by listening to students' comments and by reading care-
fully their shorter writing did I come more clearly to see the nature
(for students) of the reading I had assigned. True, it was about

making ethical decisions as part of everyday life. And it made an interesting point, suggesting that the ethical dilemmas of everyday life have more to do with choosing between two goods rather than choosing between a right and a wrong. As I listened to students, however, I came to see they did not find this point interesting at all and in fact didn't get it, except abstractly. They could repeat it but didn't seem to know what it meant.

What was I to conclude? The central assumption of the article was that decent people simply know the difference between right and wrong. Stealing was wrong, and a decent person, if he stole, would know that he was doing something wrong. There was no ethical dilemma here. Rather, the dilemma arose in having to choose between two goods: telling the truth to a friend (a good) as opposed, say, to a loyalty to one's company and its codes (a good). Did my students not get it because they didn't know the difference between right and wrong and thus were not positioned to grasp the dilemma of two opposed goods?

As I listened, I came to see that students were not positioned to grasp the article's primary formulation. I don't mean to say that students didn't know the difference between right and wrong and were not decent people. No, they were simply involved with ethical issues at another level entirely. As Kegan suggests, students may occupy the third order of consciousness. At that level, they are very much concerned with their own subjectivities and the subjectivities of others. This level of subjectivity seemed to me very much the ethical level at which my students were operating. They wanted to know the difference between right and wrong, and the difference was not always so clear because they were concerned very much with ethics as it relates to interpersonal issues. Students wanted to be true to their ethics but found that in interpersonal relations they could not always be true. But did that mean they had been wrong?

By listening to my students, I came gradually to see that I had made a mistake in my selection of the reading. The article I had selected, I saw more and more clearly, was aimed at decent people who were professionals and who, in relation to those professions, had absorbed a code of conduct and a sense of personal responsibility for that code. As a librarian and a decent person, one might indeed be torn between the desire to protect the privacy of library patrons (a good) and the desire of the police to gather information on a possible criminal (also a good). As Kegan suggests, the university is but one modernist institution; other institutions, for which a university degree is frequently required, may include the institutional notion of the professions. The code of a profession, by forcing one to look at the big picture or the implications of a choice for the self-image of the profession, also forces one to experience ethical autonomy. The person who is incapable of experiencing this autonomy cannot be said to act ethically.

Why I did not recognize immediately that this reading was not appropriate for my students—in their particular experiential realities—I don't know. I expect that it looked good to me primarily because I unconsciously and narcissistically responded to its most basic and modernist assumptions. I belong to a profession and have to make ethical choices in relation to it. But because I approach every assignment as a mini experiment, as a way of attempting to fathom the effects of my presentation on students, I was not caught completely flat-footed by their response to the article.

I had hoped that they might use the article to move toward the fourth order of consciousness and that the abstractions it afforded might function for them as a tool of analysis. I might have plunged on in that direction and insisted that students write "on" and "about" the article, but given my sense of their subjective reaction to it, I concluded that such a plan was useless. Instead, I rewrote the assignment, stressing that students refer to the article only when they found it useful in analyzing an ethical dilemma they had experienced. If it was not useful, they could ignore it. The results were not entirely satisfactory; personal experience was mixed with clumsy attempts to integrate portions of the article. That clumsiness, though, I recognized as partly my doing (having come better to understand what I had assigned), and overall, the results were better than those expected had I insisted on staying the course.

The Role of Self-Disclosure

I approached Epictetus as a mini experiment. Accordingly I began to form a hypothesis. What were, I wondered, the potentials in Epictetus for narcissistic wounding or self-destabilization in students who did achieve a subjective relation to his work? The first step is to assist students in achieving a subjective relation to the text; the next step is just this question. I have found, over the years, that many students have trouble, if they achieve a subjective relation, with forms of thinking that used to be called materialism. Students occasionally even become angry with such thinkers. The reasons for this anger are fairly clear; materialisms of all kinds are narcissistically wounding because they show that persons are not in control but are in fact controlled by relatively impersonal forces. I didn't see this particular potential, though, in Epictetus.

I did, however, see another. Epictetus seems to be about controlling desire. Indeed, an easy misinterpretation might be that he is really all about stomping it out completely. I don't think this is the case. But being young is in part about being overwhelmed by desires of various sorts, and from that perspective, I wondered whether my students might not see Epictetus as antidesire. That view could produce some self-destabilization of a relatively deep sort. Further, Epictetus is antimaterialistic. Indeed, a modern, relatively "hip" translation of *The Enchiridion* very much stresses that point; Epictetus is about not acquiring objects or social status, or consuming, or possessing. Rather he points out all the ways persons might lose their souls in just those pursuits. This philosophy too, if students saw and understood it at all, could be very self-destabilizing.

At one level, Epictetus's message, with its elements of antidesire and antimaterialism, seemed so potentially narcissistically wounding I wondered whether students would be able to relate subjectively to him at all. One's narcissistic allegiances are strong, and when they are challenged, one's defenses act accordingly. I believed it possible that students might simply dismiss his writings as the outdated and "totally old school" ravings of some strange Roman. In part because of this possibility, I tried, in a roundabout way, to suggest a possible relevance in Epictetus for our times. Finals, a time of great stress to all, were coming up, and I told students that reading Epictetus might have some use relative to the situation. After all, I indicated, a great deal of what he said could be found in rehashed form in the stress-management section of the local bookstore.

By presenting Epictetus in this way, I wanted to suggest for students a potential subjective relation to the material. At the same time, of course, I risked trivializing his message and limiting the potential for self-destabilization should students subjectively connect with his deeper and much less modern message. Frankly, I don't know how or whether this particular tactic worked at all. I tried another tactic relative to the issue of youth and desire. In part I was attempting to point students in the direction of what Epictetus says about desire and thus to evoke in them a possible subjective relation to it. I also attempted, by recognizing the potential for narcissistic wounding at just this level, to defuse any too intense destabilization. I said, "You know, Epictetus might not really be your cup of tea. A cup of tea, I mean, for young people. But he might be of interest to older people, like me, who are coming up against their limits."

In effect here, I engaged in what in psychoanalytic circles is called an act of self-disclosure. I even complained for a few minutes about my middle-age aches and pains. Some psychoanalysts of the more traditional sort are opposed to any form of self-disclosure (so that the analysand's transference might be facilitated); others suggest that it is impossible to avoid self-disclosure and to try to avoid it is absurd. In either case, through this act of self-disclosure, I altered the intersubjective terrain between myself and my students. I directly and purposefully called attention to the fact that I am older (going on old) than they are. In addition, I suggested that because I am old, Epictetus might mean to me something different from what it might mean to them. In a more general way, I suggested that how a person understands or relates to anything might have a great deal to do with his or her self-experience.

In one way, by pointing their attention (and mine) to the difference in our ages and the implications of that for the way we understand, I might appear to have broken the narcissistically informed identification of student with teacher and teacher with student. Indeed, that was part of my intent. I wished to say I read this text in a particular way because I am who I am. What I would like to know, so that I might understand, is how you read this text on the basis of who you are. In fact, a simple self-disclosure of this kind does not break the narcissistic identification. But it may have another effect. At such moments I may, through the act of self-disclosure, serve for some students as a stabilizing selfobject. Because of the power of the teacher, he or she may, even by saying the obvious, bring into consciousness for the student just this obvious thing. This bringing into consciousness may shift the student's self-relation to the text in however slight a way.

I have found that when I teach "materialism," I may mute students' sometimes unconscious angry response to it by acknowledging that I too find it troubling. When I teach something about social theory, conformity, and obedience, I try to teach it as troubling for me. I do not dispute that the social theorists may be right; I am no expert and not positioned to say in any particular way whether they are or aren't. But whether I am right or wrong, I can still be troubled. By engaging in this act of self-disclosure, I help those students who might also be troubled by the material to acknowledge that affective response. And because it is acknowledged and brought relatively into consciousness, students' self-relation to this affect is changed. They may, then, take up the idea of being troubled as their entryway into the material and, as a consequence, engage the material in a slightly more thoughtful way.

The Affective Response as Avenue to Subjectivity

The instructor, relative to ideation, intellection, and meaning making, has great power. The way the instructor presents the material can, on the basis of the narcissistic identification of student with teacher and teacher with student, greatly determine students' responses. I wish not to abrogate this power but to use it in a particular way, toward the creation of the writing class as transitional environment. Such a creation requires, in Kegan's terms, conceiving of the writing class as a "tricky transitional culture, an evolutionary bridge, a context for crossing over" (43). My reflections above may suggest how tricky this "transitional culture" can be. One thing though seems clear. The student will not cross the bridge from the third to the fourth order of consciousness, and the class will not function as transitional environment, if the student leaves his or her self behind. That is the hardest part, given the prevailing pedagogy, in the construction of the writing class as transitional environment.

It is easy to say to students, "I would like your subjective response" or "I would like to see how you understand." We tend to assume that students speak the same language that we do. But they don't. I know from experience that some students may interpret *subjective response* as any old random response or as "I can say anything I want to about this without being in the least accountable for what I say." The problem with the assertion "I want your subjective response" is that it presupposes for its "correct" understanding precisely the fourth order of consciousness that one is trying to teach. If students knew that, then I would not have anything to teach. But they don't.

Students are not yet aware that they have subjective responses that are their own and particular to themselves. Rather they have a subjective or narcissistically informed relation to their selfobjects that leads them to believe that those objects are reality. With that view, then, they are not interpreting in relation to their subjectivity but are simply neutrally responding to the real. And if what they are seeing is real, what else can they do but reflect it as accurately as possible, whatever it is? This view, I think, describes students' relations to their ideas, beliefs, notions, ideations, and intellections, which are experienced as real. And if they are seen as real, students are ill-positioned to "rise" to self-authorship, or to what Kegan calls an internal identity (self equals self) from which it is possible to see that what one has taken as "real" lacks any coherence or internal consistency or order. Only when one can begin to see that her or his reality is self-constructed is one positioned to see oneself as self-authoring.

To self-authorship is where I would like students to go, but I don't think I can help them make the transition if I ask them to leave their selves behind at the other side of the bridge. The most effective practical means I have found for helping students to acknowledge their subjectivities as subjectivities is to encourage them to pay attention, when reading and writing, to their affective or emotional responses. If one associates autonomy and objectivity with the "rider off the horse" (ego autonomy), then I may appear to be encouraging students to head in exactly the wrong direction. But, as I have suggested, I believe the cultivation of self-authorship is better understood as ego dominance, or the rider on the horse of the passions.

Thought, contemplation, self-reflection, and cognition—all to my mind are not somehow distinct from and certainly not superior to the affects. Thought, cognition, and self-reflection are derived from affect and represent the attempt of the self to establish a particular relation and peculiar relationship to affect. This statement seems to me transparently true. Anxiety, for example, is not just an irrational affect; it is a way of experiencing, understanding, and knowing the world. Some evolutionary biologists have gone so far as to maintain that anxiety is the necessary affective prerequisite for intelligence. I don't know whether that is true. But certainly the writing class as transitional environment presupposes that affects are ways of knowing and learning about the world that are particular in their shape and manifestation to each individual.

I do not argue that students must undergo self-destabilization, with possible attendant affects of rage, anxiety, depression, and joy, just so that they might experience these emotions. Rather, these affects are warranted as the means by which students may move to another position with respect to them. One may learn, however, by and through an affect (or understand what it has to teach) only if one is able actually to experience it. Unconscious affects (and they are always operating), as the unthought known, remain off the map of possible learning. Further, if one is to learn what an emotion has to teach, one must be able to bide with and not deny or repress it.

My writing assignments, as part of my presentation of the environment I am attempting to construct, all add up to this. I try to frame the assignment as an opportunity to bide with an affective response and to work out the implications of that response for the student's particular understanding of the material. Try to pinpoint for me, I suggest, what particular portions, down to individual sentences, of the reading seem most to have evoked or solicited a particular affective response. What, if you can say, is that particular affective response? Can you characterize it, if not for me, at least for yourself?

Please understand, I am not going to argue with your affective response. I am not going to say you were wrong to be angry or confused or upset. That is your response. Your subjectivity. An affective response is not true or false, right or wrong. It is in effect an interpretation. But understand too that I might not have the same affective response at all. In that light, try to help me understand, to the best of your ability, what there might be in your particular system of beliefs or relative to your ideas or background that would lead to your affective response. If you can do that—if you can point to the text and show me how your beliefs or notions or ideas may play a role in your particular affective response—then I am positioned to understand that response. And in the course of understanding your response, I may be able to broaden my own understanding or see a new way of interpreting the materials at hand.

Within the intersubjective terrain at least, introspection and extrospection go hand in hand. The second part of the assignment—the looking inward for beliefs or ideas or notions that might account for the affect—marks a step toward the extrospection. The affective response comes first; without it, learning, as I mean it, is not possible. But the second step, the attempt to account for the affect, means moving toward an awareness of self-authorship, toward the awareness that the affective response was not produced by the object but is the result of the various meanings one has brought, more or less unconsciously, to bear on it. The affective response marks one end of the transitional bridge; the attempt through introspection to extrospect the object marks the other.

I conceived of Epictetus as the bridge between my students and myself. At one end of Epictetus, as bridge, were the students. At their end was the possibility of affective response and, through it, the establishment of a subjective connection to his words. I was concerned that the potentials for affective destabilization and self-destabilization might be too great. If they were, students would, largely unconsciously, dismiss Epictetus's thinking and produce in their writing relatively fragmented (because of Epictetus's chunky style) regurgitation of his philosophy.

From my end of the bridge, Epictetus seemed an interesting philosopher. Furthermore, given my desire to move students to the fourth order of consciousness, there was enough in him to stimulate this possible move. Philosophers are like scientists: they both tend to overturn and call into question our more commonsense apprehensions. They tend further to view things systematically and to seek internal coherence in thought, again not typical of commonsense thinking. Possibly, then, Epictetus might afford some students, on the basis of having their beliefs challenged by his way of thinking, the opportunity to take up this particular philosophical way of thinking as a stabilizing selfobject.

One Student's Affective Response to Stoicism

Almost immediately, I hit a snag. I wanted to encourage students to respond with affects, so during a visit to the computer lab, I asked them to pick a passage from Epictetus and to cut and paste it (I had posted a copy of *The Enchiridion* on my Web site) into an e-mail to be sent to me. In addition and more important, I wanted them to indicate why they had picked the particular passage. I would then run through the e-mails, I said, and cull some to be used as a basis for our next class discussion.

Back in my office, I went over the e-mails and found:

> I don't want to read any more of this guy. I can't read a guy who says this. . . .
>
> "With regard to whatever objects give you delight, are useful, or are deeply loved, remember to tell yourself of what general nature they are, beginning from the most insignificant things. If, for example, you are fond of a spe-

cific ceramic cup, remind yourself that it is only ceramic cups in general of which you are fond. Then, if it breaks, you will not be disturbed. If you kiss your child, or your wife, say that you only kiss things which are human, and thus you will not be disturbed if either of them dies."
    This is too cruel.

I was a startled. We had just started looking at *The Enchiridion* and already here was a pretty distinct affective response. I found myself a bit troubled too. I had read *The Enchiridion* a couple of times (it isn't long) before assigning it and couldn't, for the life of me, recollect the passage the student had quoted. In fact I had to look it up in the text to confirm that it was there. I wondered why I might have missed a passage that had apparently stuck out so starkly for my student.

I was also taken aback by the particular intensity of the response. "I don't want to read any more of this guy." Was this a subjective response in the bad sense? I have struggled for some time with this sense of the word *subjectivity*. I recollect colleagues on more than one occasion arguing that what we have somehow to help students overcome is the I-like or I-don't-like response. This reaction appears to be subjectivity in the bad sense, in that it suggests a purely irrational and idiosyncratic response, one that as such cannot be argued with but inhibits students' abilities to think about the harder materials we ask them to read. In other words, in asking students to respond affectively, am I not risking the I-like or I-don't-like response and in so doing encouraging them to think with their prejudices?

I felt for a moment that by encouraging students to respond affectively, I had encouraged this student just to react with her gut. Momentarily challenged, I thought this feeling through and concluded that better the I-like or I-don't-like response than none. And if this response is at the heart of students' problems with the more difficult things we ask them to do, what is the best way to help them overcome it? I would say the answer is to ask or try empathetically to understand why a student might like or not like. Perhaps it is true: "de gustibus non est disputandum." And that might seem to suggest taste is a bad thing or, to the extent that it is not arguable, a lapse into pure solipsism.

This response seems, however, to be that of a teacher or instructor who might want to argue students out of their taste. I don't see a problem if one's goal is to understand the taste and not to argue the student out of it. For example, I do not like lima beans. If someone were to ask me why I don't like them, I could tell a fairly lengthy story about having to finish everything on my plate and the way that blossomed into a fairly intense hatred for the Jolly Green Giant. The question about my dislike of the lima bean, depending on how much time my auditor had at his or her disposal, could prove just the tip of the iceberg or the prelude to an extended disquisition on my family's eating habits and their implications for the development of my psyche. My point in telling the story, moreover, would not be to argue against people who do like lima beans but simply to afford to my auditor a deeper understanding of why I don't.

And once I had gotten over my problem with the student's I-don't-like response, I saw that she had not just said something subjective in the bad sense but had also characterized, on the basis of the passage selected, the author as cruel. Accordingly for the next class session, I printed out the student's response and read it aloud to the class. "Had anybody else," I asked, "noticed this passage? Because I sure didn't." And if so, what did they think? The discussion that followed was energetic. Some students argued, on the basis of the passage, that Epictetus's whole philosophy appeared inhuman. *Cruel* was not a sufficient word. Others disagreed.

Throughout the next two weeks of discussion on Epictetus and what and how to write about him, I kept an eye on the student who had sent the initial e-mail. She didn't say much. But given the intensity of her affective response and the discussion it had provoked, I hoped to see in her paper proof of my theory. I hoped, in other words, that her affective response might have afforded her entry into Epictetus and that the ensuing discussion might have helped to place her in a more thoughtful relationship to Epictetus and his philosophy. Instead I received the following:

The Effects of Human Loss

The first thing that came to mind while reading Epictetus was the Buddhist idea of dukkha. Dukkha means suffering. Buddhists' believe that life is dukkha. The world to them is empty; everything is made up of things of two, which will ultimately break up and cause pain (dukkha). This, to me, is very similar to the pessimistic views, which Epictetus seems to be conveying.

Epictetus says: "If you kiss your child, or your wife, say that you only kiss things which are human, and thus you will not be disturbed if either of them dies." Here, he introduces his idea that objects and people have a nature. This general nature, he says, is what we as humans should look for in everything that is important to us or makes us happy. But, can everything really be summed up in a couple of general categories?

The phrase, general nature, is very superficial. It does not take into account the deeper meaning of something, its sentimental value, or its individual worth. For example, I have a blanket that my grandmother sewed herself and gave to me on the day that I was born. Over the years, it has sustained many injuries, and she had to repair it. I always have it on my bed. It is so important to me that I will go back for it if my dorm or house is ever on fire. I would save it before anything else, excluding people of course. Epictetus would say that I was ridiculous and that it is not that one blanket that I love, but simply blankets in general. But he is wrong in my opinion because the reason I have kept the blanket for so long is because it is something that my favorite person made for me with her own two hands, and then continued to fix it when it began to fall apart.

Epictetus suggests that we control or even avoid grief. But there is nothing wrong with going through a grieving process. For many people, including myself, the process of grief is necessary to move past a life-altering event. I used to be a person who thought more like Epictetus in that I, too, tried to convince myself that death was just a part of life, and that the emotions that most people feel when someone dies like sadness, depression, and feelings of loss, had no real therapeutic value. I thought crying was the most useless action.

My attitude changed after the death of my grandmother. She was the first really close relative to die. She had been a second mom to me from day one. She would come over everyday and stay with me or be waiting for me when I got home from school while my mom was at work. I never saw a babysitter. If my parents went out, or left town, she would stay with my sister and I. When she stayed overnight, she would stay in my room and I would sleep in my sister's room. On cold winter mornings, I would always crawl in bed with her because she would always bring her electric blanket and her bed would be so warm. We would lie together, and she would tell me all kinds of stories about when she was a little girl and when my mom was young. Then we would get up and make her delicious recipe for biscuits and gravy. Only, the so-called recipe she referred to was the one in her head. I used to love watching her make it. She would throw in a pinch of this and a pinch of that. Needless to say, there isn't a person around who ever managed to make them the way she could.

She died four days after my fifteenth birthday. The odd thing was that my family decided to celebrate my birthday a couple days early that year and my grandma came to dinner with us. The next morning she had a stroke in our kitchen and went into a comma. This was one day before my actual birthday. She did not wake up after that. My mom came in with tears streaming down her face, and told me that my grandmother and my namesake had died. I did not cry. I did not even flinch. I just nodded that I heard her and kept on getting ready. I made it through, day after day, with people all around me outwardly grieving for my grandmother, all the while I was telling myself that their grief was ridiculous. I made myself believe for the longest time that it was not something to cry about because death was just a part of life and crying would not solve anything. I even made it all the way through her funeral, through people who loved her getting up and talking about her, without shedding a tear.

My emotional collapse did not come until almost two years later. I still had not cried for her death and to be honest, I never really expected to. There was no doubt that I loved my grandmother and that I missed her. I had convinced myself that she was still with me, but suddenly, this logic was not enough. I remember waking up from a dream I had about her, which naturally I could not really remember in detail. The dream got me thinking about her and I realized how much about her I had forgotten already. It killed me that I could not remember her face without a picture, or that I could not remember what the last conversation we had was about. I threw my covers back and hurled out of bed, determined to find something that would help me remember. I found myself crying hysterically while tearing up my room for cards she had given me so that I could read her thoughts or for a picture so that I could see her face. I am not sure how long this went on for, but I do know that at some point I became somewhat satisfied at what I had managed to find in my room. I crawled back in bed and went to sleep.

This one night changed my attitude, not just about death, but also about life. I realized for the first time how beneficial to the soul crying really was. I had spent so much time mocking it, and yet, here I was feeling relieved by it. Ever since that night I have felt as though I do not need convincing that she is still a part of my life. I can hear people talk about her now and not wish the conversation would end.

I am a better, more fulfilled person because of my grandmother. I truly believe that subconsciously each person in some ways has been shaped and molded by those people around them. My grandmother taught about what unconditional love really was. I could tell her anything that I had done wrong and she would make it all right with out telling my parents. She loved me for who I was. Unlike my parents, she never encouraged me to be anything that I did not want to be. She also taught me what it means to work hard, to care for others, to be generous, and most of all to be accepting and forgiving. Although I could never be the person she was, she has provided me with an awesome example, and it is for these lessons in good character and for her love that she deserves my grief and my love.

I don't think Epictetus would agree with my methods of grieving. He would say that I was on the right track to a fast healing when I was convincing myself that everything dies and that I shouldn't have felt as though my grandmother belonged to me in any way. She was simply on loan from God. I think, though, that he would have told me not just to convince myself of the temporary nature of people and things, but to really believe and understand it.

A Psychoanalytic Reading of One Student's Affective Response

As I have indicated, I approach each assignment as a micro experiment. And in light of my experiment, I anticipated this student's paper in a particular way. The conditions all seemed right for a demonstration in practice of my particular theory, a jump conceivably in the students' writing from a third-order to a fourth-order perspective. But I did not detect it here. The student didn't appear, at least, to have, after extended class discussion, in any way revised her original affective response or to have moved to a more extrospective relation to *The Enchiridion*. Epictetus was still too cruel.

On a more positive note, the student's paper clearly was not canned. She was not intent simply on showing she knew what I knew. Further, the response did appear to support my belief that the best way to respond to the I-like, I-don't-like response was to ask why. Like me, if I had been asked why I dislike lima beans, the student had written a story. And it seemed to me, if I looked closely, that the student knew what she was doing. She knew that what she was writing was not precisely what I, the teacher, wanted.

She took a risk in several ways. The paper gives signs of having been written in some haste, not typical of the student's other work for the class. Surely had she taken or had the time for an edit, she would have changed that "hurled" out of bed to "jumped." The stuff sort of comes pouring out. She mentions that she did not flinch when first told of her grandmother's death but "kept on getting ready." But for what? And why mention that "odd" thing about the celebration of her birthday being pushed forward four days?

But if the student were willing to take a risk, I had made it possible. From the very beginning, I neither assumed nor asserted that the chief goal of my pedagogy was for students to write on Epictetus academically. Rather, because I think writing academically entails a significant developmental move, I told students that I wanted them to show me, to the best of their ability, their understanding of Epictetus. Wasn't this after all what the student was attempting to do in her paper? Wasn't she attempting to explain to me why she found Epictetus cruel? If I look at her paper in this way, things begin to shift. To understand her response, I must exercise on my part a degree of empathetic understanding. Regarding the student's work as an assertion of self into the intersubjective terrain, with me at one end of the bridge and her at the other, I see much more going on in this paper than could ever be captured in the phrase "narrative of personal experience."

By responding to the student's work empathetically, I can begin to hypothesize that on first reading Epictetus, the student was reminded of her grandmother. The student had brought herself to the reading in the form of a series of memories that, given Epictetus's assertion, led her to shape those memories in a particular way. Epictetus, she seems to say, does not know what grief is. She recounts then her early memories of her grandmother, her initial inability to grieve, and finally that night when she wakes to find that the memories of her grandmother are fading. She is then overcome with grief and frantically searches her room for some mementos of her grandmother, things that might restore her memory.

What was the student looking for in her room that night but a manifestation of her grandmother, a physical selfobject? Something external that might balance her in her grief. After that night, however, the student concludes that she no longer needs convincing that her grandmother is part of her life. During the night, the student managed to face her grief and in so doing to alter her selfobject relation to her grandmother. Previously, even hearing her deceased grandmother mentioned in conversation inflicted on her a kind of wound. The reminder in conversation that her grandmother was no more suggests that the student as a child had developed a strong and particular selfobject relation to her grandmother.

This selfobject relation is apparent in the student's narrative. The constantly rewoven blanket takes on a particular significance as a sign of a strong attachment or narcissistic tie to her grandmother. Furthermore and more significant, the grandmother seems to have acted for the student as an "idealizable" ("a person I could never be" and "awesome") selfobject. A person who may be idealized is necessarily a person stronger and more powerful than oneself. The death of such a person, then, may be experienced as a massive disillusionment, a form of betrayal of the initial idealization. The death of the idealized object destabilizes the self that idealizes the object.

Also operating here may be a deeper and possibly more painful form of narcissistic attachment to the grandmother. The student writes, "I could tell her anything that I had done wrong and she would make it all right with out telling my parents. She loved me for who I was. Unlike my parents, she never encouraged me to be anything that I did not want to be." The student had experienced the grandmother not only as "idealizable" (someone who can carry her ideal and is worthy of it) but as narcissistically affirming of her self. Significantly, "unlike her parents," her grandmother never encouraged her to be anything she did not want to be.

If I understand the student's response in this way, I can perhaps get to the core of her feeling that Epictetus, in his recommendations for the avoidance of grief, was cruel. As a narcissistically mirroring and idealizable selfobject, the grandmother had functioned as a person who affirmed the student in her being or simple existence. As such, the grandmother, in her particular attentions and affections, affirmed the student's narcissistic sense of being in some way special in her simple uniqueness. There was nothing the student had to do to be special; she had only to be who she was. No doubt the grandmother gave her granddaughter a great gift. Epictetus's claim finally was cruel because it seemed to deny to the student not so much the specialness of her grandmother but the specialness the grandmother had afforded the student as a particular selfobject.

To bring this awareness into consciousness, though, is not easy. It is hard to think that one is grieving not for the other who is lost but for oneself, for the loss of a selfobject, which allowed one to experience oneself in a particularly precious way. Coming to see, indeed, that the other was just a human being like oneself would mean, in this instance, losing the sense of specialness that arose from the other because she was "idealizable." But when I look at the last paragraph of the student's work, I have to wonder whether she is not close to this awareness.

> I don't think Epictetus would agree with my methods of grieving. He would say that I was on the right track to a fast healing when I was convincing myself that everything dies and that I shouldn't have felt as though my grandmother belonged to me in any way. She was simply on loan from God. I think, though, that he would have told me not just to convince myself of the temporary nature of people and things, but to really believe and understand it.

The student starts this paragraph by apparently separating herself from Epictetus's view of grieving. She feels that according to him, her form of grieving was not on the right track. But then she writes, "She was simply on loan from God." This sentence stands out like a sore thumb. It's straight from Epictetus, but she does not attribute the saying to him. Who is speaking it? The student perhaps? Given this ambiguity, the "though" in the next sentence doesn't make much sense.

Or perhaps it does, since she appears in that last sentence to contradict or qualify the first sentence of the paragraph; perhaps that is the referent for "though." No, she seems to say, Epictetus was asking her not simply to convince herself of the temporary nature of people and things "but to really believe and understand it." I wonder whether this line—"to really believe and understand it"— does not suggest that the student does understand Epictetus, that coming to believe and then to understand the temporary nature of people and things is not the same as understanding that we are all simply human beings.

When I read the student's work in this way, in a more empathetic light, as an attempt to express how she understood Epictetus, I found myself less disappointed (indeed, less concerned) that the student had not risen to the fourth order of consciousness and expressed herself in more academic language. With this reading in mind, I wondered whether I had not in fact achieved one of my goals: to present to students the possibility of the act of writing as self-restorative. My more empathetic reading suggested that the student had indeed been destabilized by reading Epictetus at a fairly significant level. The act of writing, while appearing in some ways at least to be a rejection of Epictetus, may then have served as an act of stabilization or restoration of the self. Through writing, the student asserted—as an independent center of initiative—her own self-relation to Epictetus as it arose from her experience of grief. And as I have hinted, the last paragraph of the paper suggested that the student had perhaps begun to revise her initial response to Epictetus. She seems close at least to having internalized the assertion that made her think he was cruel.

The Tables Turned, or My Narcissism

My rereading of the student's paper about Epictetus leaves me with a problem. Through it I am better able to understand why the student experienced Epictetus as cruel. But if I am to view the writing class as intersubjective, this deeper understanding must prompt me to ask why I did not—and still don't—experience Epictetus's assertion as cruel. The fact is I simply don't feel it. This lack of feeling might be because I continue to read him wholly academically. From an academic perspective, I am not so much concerned with my affective response to his writing as I am with what I think he is saying. I am intrigued especially with his distinction between things a person can control and things a person can't. I saw, almost as soon as I began to teach *The Enchiridion*, a curious and provocative overlapping between what Epictetus was saying and my own interest in psychoanalysis.

From a psychoanalytic perspective, Epictetus could be easily (mis)interpreted as being all about the relation of the self to its objects. If one does not wish to experience the grief and loss or narcissistic wounding that comes from a narcissistic fusion with objects, the best course of action, he seems to say, is to become as mindful as one can of one's limits. If one can become mindful of these limits, one may at least minimize the narcissistic wounding that attends investing self in objects that one necessarily cannot control or that might be beyond one's grasp. This interpretation is fine and dandy, if one can be mindful or if one actually believes that the exercise of reason in this way can be self-stabilizing. That reason did function for Epictetus in this way seemed apparent. In the face of the narcissistic wounding built into the very fabric of life and the transience of things, the ideal of the philosopher functioned for Epictetus as his fundamental selfobject.

I do not doubt that philosophies and theologies can and do function for people as stabilizing selfobjects. But this understanding of how philosophies may function is based on the fundamental assumption that people are largely unconscious and mostly irrational. I had to ask: Was Epictetus's philosophy then the rationalization of a particular pathology or set of defenses maintained to ward off any attachment to objects? Could my inability to understand my student's response be in any way related to my sharing with Epictetus a particular pathology? If so, my narcissistically infused and maintained relation to that pathology would necessarily limit the range of my empathy. I began accordingly to psychoanalyze Epictetus's philosophy.

In the language of object relations, Epictetus appears fixed in the "schizoid position." Of the schizoid type, Harry Guntrip writes,

> The schizoid intellectual is a particularly important type. . . . Highly abstract philosophy seems unwittingly designed to prove Descartes' dictum, "Cogito, ergo sum" . . . the perfect formula for the schizoid intellectual's struggle to possess an ego. A natural human being might be more likely to start from "I feel therefore I am." (65)

Viewed from this perspective, Epictetus's highly abstract philosophy, arising primarily from the absolute distinction he attempts to make between things in a person's control and things that are not, acts as a form of selfobject by and through which the schizoid struggles to feel he or she has an ego or sense of self.

Why does the schizoid lack a strong sense of self in the first place? The answer to this question, if one attempts to respond to the whole of the technical literature, is very complicated, but these remarks by Guntrip can give an overview:

> When you cannot get what you want from the person you need, instead of getting angry you may simply go on getting more and more hungry, and full of a sense of painful craving, and a longing to get total and complete possession of your love object so that you cannot be left to starve. Fairbairn arrived at the view (1941) that *love made hungry* is the *schizoid* problem and it rouses the terrible fear that one's love has become so devouring and incorporative that love itself has become destructive. (24, Guntrip's emphasis)

In light of these remarks, one may sense in the following passage by Epictetus something perhaps less Stoic and more pathological:

> Remember that in life you ought to behave as at a banquet. Suppose that something is carried round and is opposite to you. Stretch out your hand and take a portion with decency. Suppose that it passes by you. Do not detain it. Suppose that it is not yet come to you. Do not send your desire forward to it, but wait till it is opposite to you. Do so with respect to children, so with respect to a wife, so with respect to magisterial offices, so with respect to wealth, and you will be a worthy partner of the gods. (19)

This might seem like good Stoic advice if indeed all good things come to him who waits. But the passage takes on a different coloration if viewed as a defensive rationalization designed or intended to keep out of conscious reach a desire so hungry that it would eat or incorporate everything. But the repressed will return, and following the idea of the schizoid, one could argue that Epictetus's philosophy itself evidences a desire to incorporate everything into its intellectual machine.

But, begging the reader's patience, let's take this analysis one step further. I have wanted to suggest so far that my selection of Epictetus as reading material for my students may not have been as innocent as I had initially thought. Yes, I had wanted to use Epictetus in a particular way and I was conscious of the implications of the reading for my students. But I was not wholly conscious, I believe, of my possible unconscious identifications with his view, as myself possibly a schizoid type.

I am not saying anything is wrong with this unconscious identification. Rather I accept that it is how people do read, in relation to their own particular narcissistic attachments to selfobjects. There is no magic wand or secret potion by which one can somehow bring straight from the unconscious to the conscious one's possible narcissistically informed identifications. The creation of the writing class as empathetic holding environment is a process, in other words, for both students and instructor. If the instructor wishes, to create such an environment, she must try to pay attention to the way that her own subjectivity, particularly since she is the instructor, may intersect with and form the intersubjective space between teacher and student. Students may, in other words, prove good readers of the instructor's unconscious identifications. While one's own narcissistic identifications may not be apparent to oneself, they may be glaringly apparent to someone who does not share these particular identifications. I should have been aware of this possibility when one student jokingly said in class discussion, "You better not criticize Epictetus. He [me, the instructor] thinks he is right."

This student may have seen or known me better than I knew myself. I had not fully grasped my position as my position, and indeed, there is no way to grasp it except through interaction with one's students. My inability to grasp empathetically my student's position had opened a gap or void in the intersubjective terrain, and I took the effort to fill it. The result was an increased understanding for me of my subject position relative to the materials, and an increased understanding of the potential implications of the readings for my various students. Finally, I noticed a possible identification between my psychoanalytic approach to the classroom and the possibility that I was teaching, through the psychoanalytic approach, an "ethic."

The psychoanalyst Carlo Strenger writes,

> The psychoanalytic ethic is stoic: We must accept the limits of our power. Paradoxically, fantasies of omnipotent repair of early damage weaken the individual. By endowing us with magical powers to change the past, they perpetuate the terrors of childhood. These fantasies deny us the only freedom human beings are capable of: conscious, lucid acceptance of limitations, which allows us to actualize our realistic potentials. (55)

I think Strenger's assertion is debatable. I am not convinced, for example, that Kohut's self psychology suggests it is ever quite possible to "lucidly accept one's limitations." Still, whether or not it is ever quite possible, acceptance of one's limitations might be the goal. Certainly, too, implicit in Kohut's notion of the self is the idea of actualizing one's potentials, even though fully actualizing them may never be possible. Thus, according to Kohut, the plight of modern humanity is tragic. But how can one live with that realization? Perhaps by becoming Stoic?

The "I-Response" Paper

In the foregoing examination of a unit devoted to the "teaching" of Epictetus, I wanted to give some sense of the back-and-forth between student and teacher, the dialectic inherent in the classroom as transitional environment. I framed the assignment in a particular way based on my experience and my particular psychoanalytic theory; I had certain expectations about how students might respond. Students' responses led in turn to a deeper understanding of the implications of the assignment for them and, just as important, led me to a deeper understanding of my particular self-relationship to the assignment, to what the assignment said about me and my relationship to psychoanalytic theory.

In my description of this environment, I have wanted not to be prescriptive. I have wanted to remain true to Kohut's insight that what one does, relatively to the development of others, might not be as important as who one is. In my own experience at least, the feeling that I must do certain things and do them in certain ways has not always led me to a deeper contact with who I am. The obverse has been the case. Trying to do what I felt I had to do, in relation to institutional requirements and sometimes in response to composition theory, has led me away from my particular responses to my students and from my own insights.

With these qualifications in mind, I suggest one thing that must be done before beginning construction of the writing classroom as transitional environment. Students should be encouraged to use the "I" in their writing. Much more is implied here than simply giving students permission to break a rule of standard academic discourse. This is the tip of the iceberg, or, if you will, simply the key to possibly opening the door to the transitional environment. Nancy Welch describes her efforts to help an older, returning student write an essay on *Moll Flanders*. Across the bottom of the assignment page, the instructor for the course had written in bold, "This paper is not about you." By inviting the "I" into student writing, though not absolutely insisting on it, I say the opposite. This paper is about you, about how you understand what you have read and what has been discussed in class.

At the same time, I see encouragement of the use of the "I" as part of an academically oriented writing classroom. The apparent antinomy between the "I" as something associated with personal writing and the elimination of the "I" as a sign of academic writing is unfortunate and misleading in relation to an understanding of the writing class as transitional environment. "I" writing may appear more egocentric or narcissistic and thus lacking in the power associated with knowledge claims of academic writing. But this difference does not mean that academic writing is not narcissistically informed. Learning to write within disciplinary constraints may eliminate the overt appearance of the "I," but the resultant writing style should not lead us to conclude that the writer has avoided an enormous narcissistic investment in mastering those disciplinary constraints.

The difference between the academic writer and the beginning student writer is simple. The former has narcissistically invested in disciplinary constraints and rhetorical conventions of academic writing, and the latter has not. That the former avoids use of the "I" should not lead one to conclude that the self-relation of the writer to the discipline is not narcissistically informed. That a person might use the "I" should not lead to the conclusion either that the writer is narcissistic in the sense of being egocentric or having a limited or only personal view of the world. This is not to say, of course, that the attachment of the "I" writer to what he or she writes is not narcissistically informed. Of course it is. What sort of writing isn't narcissistically informed, in some way moved ahead, by the vital psychological energies of the individual writer?

From a psychoanalytic perspective, there is no contradiction between the academically oriented writing classroom and encouraging students to use the "I." But encouraging the "I" does not mean students should write "expressively" or "from personal experience."

Rather, since I conceived of the writing classroom as a transitional space by which students can better understand the demands of academic writing, I encourage students to read academic materials and to write about them from their particular "I-position," whatever that might be. In effect, I ask students to write about their unique self-orientation to the materials at hand. In practice, this orientation may—but not necessarily—mean that students express their opinions or draw on personal experience as a way of presenting their particular I-position.

I am not sure what name precisely to give to the kind of writing I receive from my students. It is not wholly personal, nor is it wholly academic. But more important than its name is the psychological purpose such writing may serve. The movement into the university and its particular ways of knowing is inherently destabilizing for beginning students. A developmental movement is enjoined, but because this destabilization is not recognized or adequately understood, students are left pretty much to manage the passage on their own.

When I ask students to write about academic works from their I-position, I hope to achieve two intimately related things. First, I hope to better understand the kinds of turbulence and instability that students might experience in coming to grips with academic theory. Second, I hope that the student, in and through the act of writing, can achieve an at least momentary self-stabilization relative to the narcissistic wounding or destabilization involved in engaging the work.

Clearly the realization of these hopes is dialectically related. I cannot begin to understand and adjust my pedagogy accordingly if I have no idea what sort of turbulences may be awakened by the developmental move. I am not a mind reader. Students must give me some idea. The barriers to the expression of these ideas are multiple. First and foremost is the traditional student-teacher relationship. When the teacher is the one-who-knows, the student is the one-who-doesn't, and given that relation, students are likely to ignore or repress their self-relation to the object of study. But this self-relation is precisely the one thing the student might know with confidence, and knowing it would appear critical for the student in coming better to understand not simply his or her self but the subject matter. Unless, in other words, the student can come to know his or her self-relation *to* the object of student, I do not see how the student can extrospect the object of study, to come to see or hold it as something distinct *from* the self. And if this extrospection cannot be done, then, the student remains in a relative unconscious and narcissistic fusion with the object of study.

If the student remains in a form of narcissistic fusion with the subject, then he or she cannot make the developmental move. He or she is simply stuck in a nonreflective relation to the object. When, then, I encourage students to express their I-position, I see such encouragement not as a move away from the world of academic writing or academic theory but as a means of assisting students to engage that world in ways meaningful to themselves. If I am to assist students in this way, I must also attempt, in the way I present myself and construct my assignments, to suggest that my primary goal is not to judge or correct their responses but to understand them to the best of my ability.

For example, I had students read passages from Karen Horney's *Our Inner Conflicts,* in which she presents three primary character types. I was aware from previous experience that some students would have trouble with the very notion of *three* types. Surely, they would say, there are more than three types. When this claim arose, I did not dispute it. In fact, I agreed and brought in another book that had, as I showed the students, five types. What I was attempting to do, through this and a number of other maneuvers, was to show students that I recognized the justice of their claims and respected their self-relation to the material. Through this demonstration of understanding, I hoped to move students beyond this particular objection to a point at which they were able to engage the material *as a theory,* not as something that accurately represented the real but as something that created meaning.

Still, on one of my rough-draft days, I happened to visit two groups of students back to back, the primary spokesmen for which indicated that they felt what Horney had to say was "bullshit."

Taken somewhat aback, I addressed the class as a whole, described the objection I heard, and asked whether most felt I should stop assigning the works of Horney to future classes. I was open, I said, to hearing, since as a teacher I had no desire to assign to students something that most found to be simple nonsense. Surprisingly, a number of people said that what Horney had to say was not nonsense and that indeed what she had to say was quite interesting. I left it at that.

Still one student, in the first line of his paper, did declare that what Horney said was "bullshit." Who is this person, he wanted to know, to say such things about people? He must have had second thoughts, because the paper was followed by an e-mail apologizing for the "b-word." He hoped, he said, that he had not insulted me because he knew I liked Horney. I wrote back that he should not be concerned because I was not insulted.

Who the heck is this person, Karen Horney, to say such things? I know, because I have read psychoanalysis. Karen Horney is one of the "grandmothers" of psychoanalysis, along with Anna Freud and Melanie Klein. How could my student have known any of this? He had not read psychoanalysis, off and on, for twenty years as I have. And I was not insulted by what he did not know about my knowledge, because I know that my attachment to psychoanalysis, as a body of knowledge, is narcissistically informed.

Ten or fifteen years ago, the writing courses I taught included a three-week section on poetry. I didn't, given my psychoanalytic outlook and my reading about reader response, teach poetry per se or poetry as a kind of body of knowledge. Instead, I called the little reader I compiled *Fear of Poetry*. I worked hard putting that little reader together. It had no more than thirty poems that I had culled from multiple anthologies. I had wanted to find poems I felt students might understand; they were to contain no Latin, Greek, or abstruse allusions to other poetry or even other works of art. They were to be in plain language, as I put it to myself, and to embody a complex emotional experience, one in which, epistemologically, one might locate ambiguity or paradox. I compiled this reader because I wanted students to overcome their fear of poetry as something imbued with impenetrable deep meanings and to locate some shard of their own experience in it.

One day, though, as I was thumbing through my poems, all in blue ink back in the days when there were still mimeographs, and reflecting on them, I realized that I should instead title my little collection *Me.* Who was the single author most represented in my little collection but that solitary, lonely, grousing, and pretending-to-be-tough narcissist Philip Larkin. And Larkin is the classic narcissist. Surely someone has written an article, "Philip Larkin: Narcissist." And what of those Roethke poems or that one by Gunn about a person trapped in a prison? Why, a student with a background in psychoanalysis or just a general interest in psychology might have been able to diagnose me pretty well on the basis of those poems. All that was needed was for me to throw in a couple of scatological poems by Swift and the picture would be pretty complete. I felt, sitting there, looking at my "me anthology," a little embarrassed and exposed.

My point is that what we teach, whether something disciplinary or more personal like a little collection of poems, is narcissistically informed and says something more or less obliquely or indirectly about who we are as persons. When I am teaching well, what I am most teaching is me—not the "compleat" me, which would be socially inappropriate and, in any case, impossible, since I have no grasp of the complete me, for the simple reason that I am not done yet. But what I can teach is that me who has gone through to the end of the educational system, who can understand Kant, at least empathetically, and who has some inkling of what is intended by postmodernism. And I can teach these things as they are embodied in and through my subjectivity.

My student apologized *to me,* not because he didn't think Horney wasn't bs but because he had sensed my subjective relation to what she says. The student knew I liked what she had to say. And what was I going to do about that; pretend, in the name of some specious notion of objectivity, that I didn't like it? Not that I consider her writings the be-all and end-all, but she does write clearly about important things. And what might have been accomplished by pretending to objectivity? Nothing but the reduction of her thought to academic irrelevance. As it was, the student, having sensed my subjective relation to the material and that his own relation to it was not one of "like," decided, for the purposes of his paper, to set aside his own feelings about Horney and to use what she had to say. In the course of doing so, he wrote a decent paper, one that showed he understood her work in some basic ways, whether he liked it or not.

So, in the end, I have trouble with the dualism of academic and personal writing because I don't think there is anything but personal writing, in that broad sense of writing as emanating from some "individual subject." Where else could it come from? Discourse does not construct itself, at least so far; I do not think it is being generated by a computer. And to think of discourse as something self-generating is to construct, in our heads at least, some monstrous implacable machine. And if this is how one conceives discourse, then one might feel, if one wishes to insert oneself into it, that one may well have to become not "someone" but "something" that one is not.

I do not deny that discourse and discourse conventions have an institutional and social life of their own. Certainly they do, and some of them even receive government funding. But I am speaking of something more psychological and sometimes lost beneath the burden of "other-thinking" that goes into inserting oneself into the discourse. Much is gained, of course, by inserting ourselves into discourse. Parents help their children do it when they teach them to say "thank you," and not only to say it but "to say it like they mean it." A good deal is gained by such behavior, both in the long term and in the short term. One may be praised for saying "thank you." But good parents, both Winnicott and Kohut suggest, are most helpful when they teach what must be taught without destroying or putting into imbalance the child's narcissism, or sense, as Winnicott puts it, that he or she is still, at some unconscious level, "the creator of the world."

What the university, however, in its particular epistemologies, most teaches is that this is *not* true. At the level of cognition and intellection, it asserts, "No, you did not create the world. You did not make it. It makes you. Right down and into basic ways you think about yourself and the world, you are made." This lesson is a valuable one and should be taught. But the university is not helpful in the way that it teaches this lesson. I, however, want to be helpful and believe I can be within the limited confines of the writing classroom. I am a teacher of writing. I work in a murky realm somewhere between the demands and epistemologies of disciplinary constraints and the subjectivities of students as they attempt to take up and absorb the necessarily disturbing import of these disciplines and their epistemologies.

And I think I can be most helpful by accepting that what I teach is primarily just "me." That acceptance changes in fundamental ways my relationship to the knowledge or expertise I might afford. I have to admit to myself that if I am just teaching me, the things I take to be knowledge are probably narcissistically informed self-objects that might help stabilize me but may be of little use to anyone else. Further I have no way to overcome my narcissism. I am always surprised that I am surprised when, for example, students sometimes reject what I have them read as nonsense. How many times do I have to learn that particular lesson? I have learned it many times, but I always seem to forget. That's my narcissism, I suspect.

The I-response paper? It's not a particular kind or type of writing but an attitude or rather the self-experience of the writer. This writing directly or indirectly, consciously or unconsciously, says, "No one is in direct contact with reality." The reality of the particular self is mediated by the quality of its complex and sometimes contradictory relations to the real. The self has a hard time knowing itself because that would mean knowing the means by which it knows. But most of this knowledge lies in the unconscious, at the level of the "unthought known." To even begin to know this means entering the realm of "intersubjectivity" and discovering that the meanings one has discovered were created (sometimes very long ago and under circumstances that now can never be changed). But this is who one is. And knowing that may allow one to experience oneself as an idiosyncratic maker of meaning. This work is hard but worth doing because, through it, one may experience the truth of oneself and perhaps communicate it to others.

5 / Departing Thoughts: The Self-Restoration of the Writing Instructor

One reads something of the sort I have written here not just to learn but to be affirmed. Or, to put the matter somewhat more dialectically, one is able to learn to the extent that one feels affirmed. In that light, I certainly hope that what I have had to say here about the teaching and learning of writing may be experienced by my fellow instructors of writing as affirming—of their selves as teachers of writing. If, though, I have not made myself clear, I will say that I find the teaching of writing a highly complex, mysterious, frustrating, and rewarding process. It has afforded me the privilege of working with young people and, through that work, the ongoing opportunity to learn more about what is going on "out there." More important, it has offered me the opportunity to experience myself as affirmed in who I am at the deeper levels of my self.

Who I am, of course, is much more than simply an "instructor of writing." Such is the case, no doubt, with all instructors of writing. But being one of them has allowed me to feel that I am involved in a significant and meaningful activity. As I sometimes say, "I believe in education." This belief amounts to a self-assertion, and since it is, as Kohut reminds me, it makes me vulnerable. I may have and assert my belief only at the risk of having that belief not confirmed and affirmed. Indeed, I find myself, in almost daily ways, disillusioned by the conception of education that informs activities of the institution that supports me. Simply put, institutions of higher education are not educating at all, at least as I mean it.

Further, at a time when institutions of higher learning seem to be selling themselves more on the basis of the recreational facilities they afford than on education, students seem less interested in education as I mean it. They—especially the middle-class students that I teach—see education as an avenue to career. Every class is just another set of units toward graduation. And that is something I very much understand. But what if, as I have previously asked, students really want, at relatively unconscious levels, knowledge, not as means to acquire the status of an expert in this or that but as a step toward wisdom? By *wisdom* I mean the psychological wherewithal, at the level of intellection and cognition, to understand, make sense of, and obtain meaning from the bumps and bruises that necessarily attend the movement into career.

As I said, being an instructor in writing allows me to do something meaningful. And certainly, the meaning I find in the activity could be the result of my own narcissism: to think of myself as involved in the development of wisdom! What could be more highfalutin and self-important? Perhaps, indeed, I need this ideal to sustain me. But, in attempting in my classroom practices to implement this ideal, I find myself—no doubt because of the way I shape the classroom environment—believing that many students do want something more out of their educations than simply a career. They are, as I have said, at an important juncture in their lives; they are destabilized and they are looking for something. And it lies within the power of the writing instructor to begin to shape what that something might be.

The way, as I have argued, to begin to shape this something or even, for that matter, to begin to conceive of something there to be shaped lies in the attempt to conceive of the writing class as transitional environment. Unless, in other words, one conceives of students as involved in a significant psychological transition at the levels of cognition and intellection, one is not likely to be aware of the trials and tribulations that students may undergo as they make this transition. Furthermore, if one does not conceive of one's students as being in a transition, one is not likely either fully to fathom the degree of power that instructors do have. One may use this power to maintain the traditional shape of the power imbalance between teacher and student or to alter that traditional shape. The writing class as transitional environment does not mean that one abandon one's power but rather that one recognize it and use it toward the end of understanding and recognizing students' ongoing, if largely unconscious, psychological activity.

If one is able to recognize this activity, one may begin to read students' writing in a different way, as the attempt to restore the self in relation to what it has learned. Students' apparent failures to rise to academic writing or to master theory through analytic application may be understood, as I have put it, as arguments for the self. Poor writing, in some instances at least, may arise not from a lack of motivation or a simple inattention to the work but from quite the opposite. The student may well be engaged and involved, but in ways that lead to disruptions in self-stability. The potentials for this disruption may be turned dialectically to good use. If one is able to convey to students that part of one's job is to understand the way they are affected by their encounters with academic writing and with theory, one may encourage students to look at and to bring out into the open, in class discussion and in their written work, their more affective and slightly submerged responses.

If students are able to regard their more affectively charged responses as indicators of their self-relations to the materials at hand, they may then be able to experience the act of writing as potentially self-restorative, not as an exercise in self-denial or falsity but as an assertion of the self. Such responses in writing do not mean a retreat from the academic universe, from its epistemology or its conceptions of knowledge. Rather it represents another and more effective way of teaching these things by affording students the opportunity better to understand the implications of such knowledge for the experience of their selves. For some students more than others, regarding the "world" and, as part of that world, one's self from a theoretical or disciplinary perspective entails an experience of self-objectification. This experience, since it entails a degree of narcissistic wounding, may prove a difficult experience to deal with or learn from. But if students are encouraged to pay attention to their affective responses (no matter how remedial or "stupid" they might appear), students may deal with them and begin better to understand the function of theory in the intellectual life.

Speaking now from the position purely of my narcissism, I find this particular vision of the writing classroom self-affirming. As a person well into mid-life, I find myself *somewhat* less concerned with where I will be than with what I will leave behind. What I will leave behind in part will be the thousands of students who have passed through classes I have taught over the last twenty-five years. I don't fancy that these thousands of students remember me any more than I remember any one of them. But I have approached each class with the sense that part of my job—indeed, the central part—is to change minds. I have done that because I believe a changing world requires changing minds. The problem may be, however, that the changes facing young people today outstrip the capacity of any one mind to comprehend. If that is the case—and I believe it is—then more weight than ever is put on the self, on the individual's particular design as that which must serve as the fuel and the guide to self-assertion and action.

The current university pedagogy is doing nothing to address this problem. Indeed, it contributes to it by presenting knowledge as a commodity. As a result, students will seek answers wherever they can find them, in dogma, in ideology, and in those diverse self-concepts or identities afforded by the consumer society. And students—I should say people—will take up these things as sustaining self-objects while the underpinnings of traditional society unravel, when the very notion of family, for example, becomes problematic, or when the activities of the species appear to threaten the ecological system that sustains the whole. The possibility of disintegration anxiety that Kohut identifies with the plight of modern humanity would appear even more a distinct possibility in the condition characterized as postmodern.

In light of these conditions, the idea that I might, through the implementation of my particular pedagogy, assist students in their self-development is for me narcissistically affirming. As Winnicott argues, a greater and more significant divide, even than that between the classes, may be division between those people who are capable of self-development and those who are not. I cannot of course assist those who cannot develop, but I would be doing less than my job if I did not try to assist those that can. That, I suppose, is what I would like to leave behind, to believe that I have assisted some young people in locating their selves and recognizing the importance of knowledge for the development of that self. For ultimately, the ability of the society as a whole to recognize and deal creatively with the challenges that confront it will depend on just such young people.

Works Cited

Bartholomae, David. "Inventing the University." *When Writers Can't Write.* Ed. Mike Rose. New York: Guilford, 1985. 134–65.

———. "Writing Assignments: Where Writing Begins." *FForum: Essays on Theory and Practice in the Teaching of Writing.* Ed. Patricia L. Stock. Upper Montclair, NJ: Boynton/Cook, 1983. 300–12.

Bascal, Howard A., and Kenneth M. Newman. *Theories of Object Relations: Bridges to Self Psychology.* New York: Columbia UP, 1990.

Bazerman, Charles. *Shaping Written Knowledge.* Madison: U of Wisconsin P, 1988.

Benjamin, Jessica. *The Bonds of Love: Psychoanalysis, Feminism, and the Problem of Domination.* New York: Pantheon, 1988.

Berger, Peter L., and Thomas Luckman. *The Social Construction of Reality.* New York: Anchor, 1989.

Birsch, Douglas. *Ethical Insights: A Brief Introduction.* Mountain View: Mayfield, 1999.

Bishop, Wendy. *Teaching Lives: Essays and Stories.* Logan: Utah State UP, 1997.

Bollas, Christopher. *The Shadow of the Object.* New York: Columbia UP, 1987.

Bracher, Mark. *The Writing Cure: Psychoanalysis, Composition, and the Aims of Education.* Carbondale: Southern Illinois UP, 1999.

Epictetus. *The Enchiridion.* Trans. George Long. New York: Prometheus, 1991.

Freud, Sigmund. "On Narcissism: An Introduction." *Essential Papers on Narcissism.* Ed. Andrew P. Morrison. New York: New York UP, 1986.

Gardner, M. Robert. *On Trying to Teach: The Mind in Correspondence.* Hillsdale, NJ: Analytic, 1994.

Gilligan, Carol. *In a Different Voice.* Cambridge: Harvard UP, 1982.

Guntrip, Harry. *Schizoid Phenomena, Object-Relations and the Self.* New York: International Universities, 1969.

Harrington, J. Anne, and Marcia Curtis. *Persons in Process: Four Stories of Writing and Personal Development in College.* Urbana, IL: NCTE, 2000.

Kegan, Robert. *In over Our Heads: The Mental Demands of Modern Life.* Cambridge: Harvard UP, 1999.

Kohut, Heinz. "Forms and Transformations of Narcissism." *Essential Papers on Narcissism.* Ed. Andrew P. Morrison. New York: New York UP, 1986.

———. *How Does Analysis Cure?* Ed. Arnold Goldberg. Chicago: U of Chicago P, 1984.

————. "Introspection and Empathy." *The Search for the Self.* Ed. Paul Ornstein. Vol 3. New York: International Universities, 1990.

————. *The Restoration of the Self.* New York: International Universities, 1977.

————. *Self Psychology and the Humanities.* Ed. Charles B. Strozier. New York: Norton, 1985.

Laing, R. D. *The Divided Self.* Baltimore: Penguin, 1965.

Le Doeuff, Michele. *The Philosophical Imaginary.* Trans. Colin Gordon. London: Athlone, 1989.

Naeem, Shahid, et al. "Biodiversity and Ecosystem Functioning: Maintaining Natural Life Support Processes." *Issues in Ecology.* 18 July 2001 <http://esa.sdsc.edu/issues4.htm>.

Papoulis, Irene. "Subjectivity and Its Role in 'Constructed' Knowledge: Composition, Feminist Theory, and Psychoanalysis. *Into the Field: Sites of Composition Studies.* Ed. Anne Ruggles Gere. New York: MLA, 1993.

Qualley, Donna. *Turns of Thought: Teaching Composition as Reflexive Inquiry.* Portsmouth: Boynton/Cook, 1997.

Sartre, John-Paul. *The Psychology of the Imagination.* New York: Philosophical Library, 1948.

Spellmeyer, Kurt. "Out of the Fashion Industry: From Cultural Studies to the Anthropology of Knowledge." *College Composition and Communication* 47 (1996): 424–36.

Strenger, Carlo. *Individuality, the Impossible Project: Psychoanalysis and Self Creation.* Madison: International Universities, 1998.

Tingle, Nick. "Peter and the Monolith: A Psychoanalytic Study of a Case of Writer's Block." *JAC: A Journal of Composition Theory* 18.2 (1998): 293–308.

————. "Self and the Liberatory Pedagogy: Transforming Narcissism." *Journal of Advanced Composition* Winter 1992. 26 May 2003 <http://www.cas.usf.edu/JAC/121/tingle.html>.

Tobin, Lad. *Writing Relationships: What Really Happens in the Composition Class.* Portsmouth: Boynton/Cook, 1993.

Welch, Nancy. *Getting Restless: Rethinking Revision in the Writing Instruction.* Portsmouth: Heinemann, 1997.

Williams, Patricia. *The Alchemy of Race and Rights.* Cambridge: Harvard UP, 1991.

Winnicott, D. W. *Home Is Where We Start From.* New York: Norton, 1986.

————. *Human Nature.* New York: Schoken, 1988.

————. *Playing and Reality.* London: Travistock, 1985.

Žižek, Slavoj. *The Žižek Reader.* Ed. Elizabeth Wright and Edmond Wright. Oxford: Blackwell, 1999.

Index

desire, 24, 123
destabilization, 72, 153; challenge of
science to common sense, 48–
50; developmental move and, 7–
9, 13–14, 145; double, 69; self-
destabilization, 50–55, 122–
23; self-reflexivity and, 86–88;
shame, embarrassment, and humiliation, 89–93, 105–6
determinate negation, 21
development, 154–55; capacity to conform and, 102–7; design of self
and, 6–7; female vs. male, 37–38
developmental move, 6–9, 39; destabilization and, 7–9, 13–14, 145;
to fourth order of consciousness,
16–18, 47, 71–72, 97; narcissism
and, 31–33; self-relation to object of study, 145–46
discourse, as term, 112. *See also* academic discourse
doing, 114–15
domination, structures of, 39–40
doubt, 48
drives, 24–25
durable categories, 48

education, as extension of mother-infant dyad, 25–26
"Effects of Human Loss, The" (student paper), 131–34
ego, 24, 61
ego autonomy, 60–63, 126
ego dominance, 60, 62, 126
embarrassment, 89–93, 105–6
empathy, 4–5, 10, 23, 110
Enchiridion, The (Epictetus), 122,
128–29
environment, supportive, 2–3, 23–25
Epictetus: psychoanalysis of, 139–43;
writing assignments on, 115–17,
122–24, 127–28

essayistic reading, 85
Ethical Insights: A Brief Introduction
(Birsch), 38–39
ethics, 5, 85, 119–21; of care, 38–39
everyday life, 48–49, 93–94
existential viewpoint, 99
extrospection, 37, 62–64, 68, 72, 85,
127, 146

Fear of Poetry (assigned reading),
147–48
feminism, modernist self and, 36–42
fourth order of consciousness, 47, 89;
craft approach and, 57, 59; and
language, 68–69; self-reflexivity
and, 84–85; transition to, 16–
22, 47, 71–72, 97. *See also* consciousness; third order of consciousness
freedom, 84, 112
Freire, Paulo, 41, 86–88
Freud, Sigmund, 24, 25, 33
furor, 76–77. *See also* narcissistic rage

Gardner, M. Robert, 76–80
generalizations, 43
Gilligan, Carol, 37–38
Giroux, Henry, 59
grading, 57–58
Guntrip, Harry, 140

Hamlet (Shakespeare), 73–75
Horney, Karen, 146–47

imaginary object, 71
In a Different Voice (Gilligan), 37–38
internal identity, 17–19, 125
intersubjectivity, 3, 40–42, 150; common sense and, 47, 53, 63–64,
84, 94; narcissistic wounding
and, 106, 110; scientific challenges to, 49–50, 53

NICK TINGLE has taught writing at the University of California–Santa Barbara since 1980. He has been an active member of his local, UC-AFT 2141, since its formation in 1987 and serves as the union representative to several senate faculty committees. He has published articles, primarily about writing pedagogy, in *JAC, College English, Composition Studies,* and *JPCS.* He has written more recently about issues of labor and adjunct faculty in *Moving Mountains* and in the online journal *Workplace: A Journal of Academic Labor.* Currently, he supervises teaching assistants and acts as academic adviser in the UCSB writing program.

Studies in Writing & Rhetoric

In 1980 the Conference on College Composition and Communication established the Studies in Writing & Rhetoric (SWR) series as a forum for monograph-length arguments or presentations that engage general compositionists. SWR encourages extended essays or research reports addressing any issue in composition and rhetoric from any theoretical or research perspective as long as the general significance to the field is clear. Previous SWR publications serve as models for prospective authors; in addition, contributors may propose alternate formats and agendas that inform or extend the field's current debates.

SWR is particularly interested in projects that connect the specific research site or theoretical framework to contemporary classroom and institutional contexts of direct concern to compositionists across the nation. Such connections may come from several approaches, including cultural, theoretical, field-based, gendered, historical, and interdisciplinary. SWR especially encourages monographs by scholars early in their careers, by established scholars who wish to share an insight or exhortation with the field, and by scholars of color.

The SWR series editor and editorial board members are committed to working closely with prospective authors and offering significant developmental advice for encouraged manuscripts and prospectuses. Editorships rotate every five years. Prospective authors intending to submit a prospectus during the 2002 to 2007 editorial appointment should obtain submission guidelines from Robert Brooke, SWR editor, University of Nebraska–Lincoln, Department of English, P.O. Box 880337, 202 Andrews Hall, Lincoln, NE 68588-0337.

General inquiries may also be addressed to Sponsoring Editor, Studies in Writing & Rhetoric, Southern Illinois University Press, P.O. Box 3697, Carbondale, IL 62902-3697.